Emily ☆

Prell day 9th September 1997.

YOUNG GERMAN ARTISTS 2

THE SAATCHI GALLERY SEPTEMBER – NOVEMBER 1997

YOUNG GERMAN ARTISTS 2
FROM THE SAATCHI COLLECTION

GRÜNFELD GURSKY HABLÜTZEL HONERT RUFF SCHÜTTE

ESSAY BY GREG HILTY

The Good and the Bad Ugly

Form & Deform

"Art and artists are not only there to unite; their far more important task is to create a *form*, to expel the ill trends and make room for the healthy to develop.... Art must not only be good, it must also be conditioned by the exigencies of the people or, rather, only an art that draws on the *Volkstum* [national tradition] as a whole may ultimately be regarded as good."
J. Goebbels in an open letter to Wilhelm Furtwängler, 1933 [1]

"When I run over the frightful catalogue of my sins, I cannot believe that I am the same creature whose thoughts were once filled with sublime and transcendent visions of beauty and the majesty of goodness. But it is even so; the fallen angel becomes a malignant devil." Mary Shelley, 'Frankenstein', 1818 [2]

Martin Honert's 1996 work 'Fata Morgana (Mirage)' is a meditation on form, vision and memory. It seeks to give form to an evanescent phenomenon which by its very definition cannot have form, which is in fact the antithesis of concrete form, demonstrating the triumph of the world of appearance and desire over the world of concrete reality. Yet far from choosing to convey this natural phenomenon through an equivalent artistic phenomenon, by playing tricks with light or with representation, Honert has endowed it with a pronounced physicality. The first focus of attention is a small sandcastle, a pathetic approximation of a palace, which sits directly on the floor. A familiar stylised representation of a set of buildings, it is also made of earth, from which real buildings are made. It functions as a tiny cell, containing in its many thousand grains the past and future memory of all built buildings. Above it, suspended between floor and ceiling, hangs a plastic apparition, the mirage of the work's title, which has the physical presence of a rather accomplished piece of night-club decor. Its irregular outline holds a painted image and the image's painted reflection. The depiction is of an idealised Arabian palace, its perfect domes, minarets and towers artificially compressed and bounded by high crenellated walls, flanked by luxuriant palms; over this vision crouches an androgynous youth, arm outstretched to make some adjustment to the ensemble. Is this figure a god, or a child on the beach, or the artist himself fashioning his work? Is he the source of the apparition or part of it and, if the latter, who is dreaming him? The answers lie somewhere in the theatrical space between the proto-castle in sand and the highly finished two-dimensional palace hovering above it.

The artists in this exhibition possess the dual urge – connected if contradictory – to give hard and fast form to, and at the same time to distort and disassemble, the realities that make up their experience of the world. Their work shows a continual interchange between the realms of the real, the ideal, and the debased. Thomas Grünfeld, Andreas Gursky, Martin Honert, Thomas Ruff and Thomas Schütte were all born in Germany in the mid to late 1950s, while Stefan Hablützel is a younger Swiss-born artist, who studied and works in Germany. Their particular engagement with reality – what can only be described as their 'will to form' – sets them and a number of their contemporaries apart from other post-war generations of German artist.

Not surprisingly, the making of German art since 1945 and its interpretation have been in large part determined by the need to deal in some way with the Nazi inheritance, whether through actively addressing it or denying it. The ideology coercively put forward by Goebbels, in spite of its rhetoric of dynamism and democracy, urged a monolithic, static view of social relationships and their portrayal in art: anything which sought to probe beneath the surface of that ideology or to deviate from its prescribed norms – whether in terms of aesthetics, psychology, sexuality, race or religion – was condemned as ugly, degenerate, and dangerous. Among the several generations of post-war German artists were many who virtually ignored the Third Reich's momentary deviation from the flow of mainstream Modernism, and who after 1945 resumed formal explorations in painting and sculpture. Others charted distinctive courses through the psychoses of their country's recent past, united by the scale of their ambition and a sense of narrative drama often verging on the theatrical. A considerable number of artists have been dogged by accusations of political ambivalence in their work, and even beyond it, especially those who felt compelled to cite the symbols of their country's dark past – Anselm Kiefer's provocative photographs of Nazi salutes, Albert Oehlen's expressive portraits of Hitler, Günther Forg's elegant evocation of totalitarian architecture – without revealing fully what status these symbols had for them. One commentator on the political minefield of post-war German art claims that even Joseph Beuys, for all his aggressively declared democratic principles, nevertheless, in the 'radical interiority' of his art, failed fully to grapple with the 'black hole' of Nazism: as openly charged a subject as the 1958 competition for an Auschwitz memorial resulted in an entry from Beuys which turned 'fact into symbol, the elements of a particular historical horror into timeless existential icons for man's cruelty to man.'[3] The fact that this comment is intended as a criticism indicates the no-win position of post-war German artists vis-à-vis their past. There was no option but for the culture to work through its guilt, while forever trying to move beyond it.

Around the late 1980s a new artistic generation began to emerge for whom the terms of discourse and reception had without doubt been transformed. There was no overt repudiation of or rupture with what had come before: the new work was just entirely different, in form and outlook more appropriate to a new age. Tempting as it is to see the fall of the Berlin Wall as a turning point, even this momentous event probably only consolidated a psychological break with the past that was already underway.

As well as the five Germans included here, one can name such artists as Katharina Fritsch, Candida Höffer, Thomas Strüth, Karin Kneffel, Michael Bach, Stephan Balkenhol, and Michael van Offen as key figures in this new generation. Their work – whether in sculpture, painting or photography – conveys a deadpan but committed realism that both engages with the surface appearance of the world around them and at the same time deliberately, if discretely, evokes the deep structures that lie beneath it, whether psychological, political, geographical, linguistic or cultural. They are interested in the singular and the generic, the individual and the mass, form and its dissolution. They invoke folk memory, neither through duty nor in detached irony, but because of its material weight in the present. They seem to share, and to convey through very different bodies of work, a sense of perpetual wonder that the world has turned out as it has.

Microcosm

"The entire planet was covered with countless signs of intelligent life. Microscopic bridges, like tiny lines, spanned every rill and rivulet, while the puddles, reflecting the stars, were full of microscopic boats like floating chips... The night side of the sphere was dotted with glimmering cities, and on the day side one could make out flourishing metropolises, though the inhabitants themselves were much too little to observe, even through the strongest lens." Stanislaw Lem, 'The Cyberiad', 1975 [4]

Andreas Gursky's 1991 photograph 'Genoa' seems to commemorate a moment of sublime tedium. Cars on a ferry sit frozen in time, forever in transit, their apparent stasis emphasised by the way the boats in the background have become part of the gridlock. An unbroken sky bears down on the scene. Some commentators have singled out this aspect of boredom in Gursky's work, as if it were a critical virtue, a deliberate achievement. Banality may well seem to characterise this work by contrast with the media-inspired saturation of energy and atmosphere of many contemporary photographers, but a more than cursory inspection shows that boredom is, as it were, the least interesting approach to the photographic explorations of Andreas Gursky.

Though drawn from the artistically unfamiliar territories of factories, shipyards, trade fairs, high-rise blocks and ski-resort restaurants, Gursky's subjects each possess an intrinsic richness of connotation, brought into the open by the range of formal devices – or, more accurately, the form-giving vision – that he employs with such consummate skill. His settings are almost invariably expansive and majestic in impact, whether portraying the Hong Kong skyline or a seemingly infinite stretch of carpet; they also almost always hold a vertiginous richness of closely-observed detail, whether capturing the hundreds of office workers within the glass cage of 'Hong Kong: Shanghai Bank' (1994) or the precise weave of the carpet in 'o.T. 1', 1993. Gursky's scenes are normally shot from above, suggesting authority and distance on the part of both photographer and viewer. The structure of his pictures is usually in tension with the structure of the subjects themselves, false frames established within the overall frame of the work, or false perspectives creating new forms out of existing ones (as in the diptych 'Hong Kong Stock Exchange', 1994).

In two of the most recent pieces shown here – 'Athens' (diptych) and 'Union Rave', both 1995 – Gursky appears to have let in what he has in the past always consciously excluded, namely a sense of atmosphere. This is conveyed in the blurry bursts of light that punctuate the cityscape, and in the grainy texture of the dance photograph. It is as if, having established a perfect crystalline clarity as his trademark, he can now deviate from it strategically so that instead of looking like a cliché of photography, each atmospheric intrusion can be seen to mean something specific. What it means in 'Union Rave' is perhaps best seen in comparison with other crowd scenes by the same artist, like the 'Hong Kong Stock Exchange' or the 'Car Show, Paris', (1993, not in exhibition): in each of these, individuals are crisply delineated, atomised units making up a greater massed whole. In 'Union Rave', by contrast, all the participants are engaged in a common purpose, listening to the same music, moving to the same rhythm, merging into an organic unit. What we see is a picture not of an event, but of an organism.

There is a clear development from the quiet observation of Gursky's earliest works from the mid- to late-1980s, which were smaller in scale and depicted scenes shot in Germany or neighbouring countries, to the more complex and exotic subjects which began to appear around 1990. Gursky's investigations of the shape of behaviour in the world today have expanded outwards from his early portrayals of the understated dramas of small town Germany to scenes which could almost happen anywhere, evidence of the rapid homogenisation of global culture on so many levels (sometimes, as indeed in 'Union Rave' which was shot in Düsseldorf, he turns back on his native land an eye more attuned to what connects it to these general patterns of behaviour). Time, too, seems more relative and fluid in the recent works, a point highlighted by critic Neville Wakefield when he writes of Gursky's focus on 'theatres of operation, of regulation, exchange and communication, where speed defies all attempts at temporal and physical measurement.'[5] This relative approach to the measurement of time, activity, and production was dramatically captured in the highly stylised film 'Koyaanisquatsi' (1983, directed by Godfrey Reggio, with music by Philip Glass), a collage of images of natural, human and manufactured profusion edited at speeds varying from the languorous unfolding of action to frenetic bursts of activity. Gursky does not allow himself such promiscuity, but is able to compress related ideas and contrasts into the radically restricted format of the large scale colour photographic print. A factory can be a site of high-speed activity or of grinding monotony, both of which moods are conveyed in the work 'Grundig, Nürnberg'. When Gursky photographs skiers, far from shooting down slopes primed for their pleasure, they trudge across vast snowy plains, watched impassively by the mountains that were there millennia before them and will remain when they have gone. The Hong Kong Shanghai Bank appears as both a hive of activity and a monolith as impressive and immovable as the pyramids treated elsewhere by the same artist. Time itself is stacked layer upon layer in the 1994 work 'Hong Kong, Grand Hyatt Park': the leisure time of people strolling through the immaculately cultivated gardens of the hotel, the work time of labourers apparently building a jetty only yards away, the transit time of the drivers on the road that separates them; and, at the top of the picture, just a little further off the coast, the international commercial time of a cargo vessel, insouciantly spewing waste into the blue waters of the bay.

Self-improvement

"His limbs were in proportion, and I had selected his features as beautiful. Beautiful! – Great God! His yellow skin scarcely covered the work of muscles and arteries beneath; his hair was of a lustrous black, and flowing; his teeth of a pearly whiteness; but these luxuriances only formed a more horrid contrast with his watery eyes, that seemed almost of the same colour as the dun white sockets in which they were set, his shrivelled complexion and straight black lips." Mary Shelley, Frankenstein[6]

Like Gursky, and in the same place at approximately the same time (Düsseldorf in the early- to mid-1980s), Thomas Ruff was also documenting his surroundings in medium-scale colour photography. His first works, begun in the late 1970s, were records of unremarkable interiors, standing in still emptiness for their inhabitants, who were never present except in framed photographs hung on walls or set on shelves.

Of little anecdotal or formal interest, these works seemed to be conforming to a self-conscious type of photography, a comment as much on the process of recording reality as on the subjects themselves. From 1981 to 1987 Ruff made several dozen small photographic bust portraits of people he knew in and around the Düsseldorf Academy, where he was a student. These first portraits were shot from a variety of angles: straight-on, three-quarters view, and from the side. The sitters could choose their own background colour. Some looked like waxwork dummies, stuck firmly in the precise era of their portrayal, betrayed by their clothes or hairstyle; others had the transcendence and timelessness of Roman portraits. Ruff continued making portraits of the same kind, and often of the same people, until 1990. But he introduced notable changes: the scale of each work was enlarged to a minimum of 200 x 150 cm ; the sitters all gazed straight ahead at the camera/viewer; the backgrounds were neutralised to white, and even the sitters' clothing became less eccentric, levelled out to a comfortably trendy Gap international-style.

These are unsettling pictures, both for what they tell you and for what they don't. What they tell you is partly conditioned by the expectations raised by their inquisitorial format, normally used for passport photographs, identity-cards or mug-shots. Ruff himself, in response to accusations that his subjects seemed devoid of personality, responded by asserting that his generation had grown up 'without candlelight', in other words in the full glare of bureaucratic and positivist scrutiny which had by the late 1970s created a paranoid society in the grip of 'Terrorismushysterie.' 'So why should my portraits be communicative,' he asked, 'at a time when you could be prosecuted for your sympathies ?' [7] These are people who have been conditioned by society not to give of themselves under observation; they are also images of 'normal' people, not actors or models trained to dissimulate, and their discomfort is palpable. While none of the portraits is a caricature, all seem to emphasise their sitters' deviation from an unreferenced perfect norm: they cannot hide a jaw too square, eyes too close together or too far apart, hair too big on a girl or too spiky on a boy. Minute failings which go unnoticed in the course of daily acquaintance or as we get to know people and develop an awareness of their multi-dimensional presence, but which compel the viewer, in William Blake's famous phrase, to 'mark in every face I meet/Marks of weakness, marks of woe.'

At the same time as they disconcert through their apparently perverse and cruel specificity, Ruff's portraits frustrate because of how little they tell us about each sitter. The general uniformity of race, age, and class distinguishes these portraits from other photo-documentary series, most notably August Sander's classic record of German archetypes, photographed between the wars. The longer you look at Ruff's portraits, the more evident it becomes that they are not actually about the people they portray; they are about the act of portrayal, about the materiality of the image-making process that reduces every subject, even the human visage, to a collection of material circumstances. Seen together in a group, the portraits become even more abstracted from their individual subjects, so that you are finally looking at almost incidental variations on a genus which happens to be human.

Ruff seems to liken the pull between the individual and the collective image, with the interplay between the represented subject and the subject of representation. He suggests, in other words, that the ease with which we, as biological or social beings, can get lost within our species or social grouping, is comparable to the homogenising effect of photographic representation itself. This becomes clearer when Ruff's 'Portraits' are seen in conjunction with the other bodies of work he has produced since the late 1980s. His early interiors were followed by the 'House' pictures, portraits of unremarkable buildings with which the artist was familiar, took for granted even, until, one by one, he decided to photograph them. Together they comprise an austere typology of the anonymous. Exhibited along with the 'Portraits' and 'Houses' in Ruff's first major public show (seen in Amsterdam, Grenoble and Zürich in 1990) was a selection from the series of 'Star' works, large-scale prints of constellations, not photographed directly but enlarged from negatives used for the standard 'Atlas of the Southern Sky'. A very different kind of found photograph is the series of ' Newspaper Photographs', captionless clichés cut out from papers, enlarged by a standard percentage, framed each the same way and hung densely on gallery walls. In 1992 Ruff, inspired by a new technique of artificially-enhanced looking witnessed in television reports of the Gulf War, completed his 'Night' series, photographs of ordinary buildings transformed into mysteriously green-tinted shadowy environments. In technique, style and scale, then, as well as in subject matter, Ruff has made highly varied groupings of images, coherent within themselves, and complementary in their sustained exploration of archetypal forms that are out there, waiting to be picked up by one means or another. Norman Bryson and Trevor Fairbrother have compared Ruff's vision to 'the sliding of a colossal zoom lens as it tracks from an unfathomable dispersion of heavenly bodies, to faces that seem plucked from the proverbial crowd, to illusory reproductions from our image-bank.' [8]

As each of Ruff's earlier series sits in a different position on the scale of first- and second-order images, and each is therefore in some sense simultaneously 'real' and 'artificial', the jump from selecting and editing images to physically amending them is perhaps not as great as might be first assumed. Ruff made the leap with his series of 'Anderes Porträts', or 'Other Portraits', made in 1994–5. Equal in scale to the standard portraits, the newer works are silk-screened where the earlier were printed photographically;

black and white instead of colour; hazy in outline instead of crisp. We recognise from the earlier work some of the faces that look out at us, but they have been merged with each other using police image-fabricating techniques. Thus in place of the harsh particularity of the original 'Portraits', the 'Other Portraits' have a more approximate and indistinct air. Androgynous hybrids, the faces they depict are without question more beautiful and mysterious than their parent images. Like real children, they manage uncannily to resemble equally both of their progenitors. The 'Other' is of course defined as that which is set against the norm, however understood: by implication it is a fluid category, subject to reconfiguring to meet the changing requirements of the norm. These 'Other Portraits' seem to be continually coming into being; they are hard to look at, hard to hold for long in the memory. In their beauty and strangeness they look like aliens or artificial beings, like representations which have resided in the imagination for so long that they have finally fully inserted themselves into the real world.

Hybridity is also the subject of Thomas Grünfeld's 'Misfits', aberrations of taxidermical talent in which the distinctive features of different species have been joined seamlessly together to produce animals unknown to nature or to textbooks. Where Thomas Ruff grafts only images together, Grünfeld grafts actual body parts: the suggestion with both is that their products are genetically rather than surgically combined. Whereas Ruff's androids seem to argue the case for their own presence though their strength and beauty, the existence of Grünfeld's 'Misfits' is more open to conjecture: it is hard to think what evolutionary imperative should have called them into being. They represent total acts of miscegenation rather than ecological fine tuning: a swan's head and neck is joined to the body of a hare, tapering back again into swans' legs, on which it stands tall and upright. Feathers blend imperceptibly with fur. A tiny deer sprouts bat's wings on its back; a bird recovers its ancestry by fusing with a fish. Often sorcery seems the best explanation for these monsters, while on occasion there seems to be a cultural, if not a biological, logic at work: the 'sheep/dog' ('St. Bernhard', 1994) for instance, seems a sensible tool for social control.

These hybrids feel as if they might actually work: just proportions are observed throughout, and the animals stand, sit or lie in quite natural positions. They are displayed in ways reassuringly familiar from museums of natural history: some are shown in single glass showcases or extended vitrines, others sit unassumingly on the floor or, as in an exhibition in Barcelona in 1995, on a patch of astroturf brought into the gallery to give an idea of the creatures' natural surroundings.

The suggested implications of the 'Misfits' – an almost limitless potential for the recombination of biological units – are certainly horrific, although with advances in biotechnology and genetic research they are also considerably nearer to reality today than when Grünfeld began working with this subject in 1990. As an artist, however, his responsibility extends to raising moral questions insofar as they overlap with aesthetic ones, but not necessarily to providing the answers. The aesthetic rationale for dealing with the subject of animal hybridity is related to the parallels drawn in the work of Thomas Ruff between the nature of reality and its means of representation: Grünfeld, however, deals in sculptural not pictorial terms. The 'Misfits' are just one, admittedly startling, aspect of an enormously varied oeuvre, again like Ruff's composed of distinct but in themselves coherent groupings. In each, Grünfeld takes a different type of object through many stages of metamorphosis. He has made wall mounted shelving units, which sometimes hold a single object of display, and sometimes act as a picture in themselves; he has made a series of upholstered pedestals, and draped fabric into hanging forms to suggest human figures; there is a range of rubber blobs that cling to the floor or wall, each seeming to hold latent energy of flow or of expansion; and, most recently, like an obsessive collector or classifier, he has filled canvases with rows of glass animal eyes of varying size, shape and colour. Through such different areas of enquiry Grünfeld attests to the apparently infinite potential of the material world – the world of the imagination, at least – to reform and to multiply itself.

Wonder

"One day, when I was oppressed by cold, I found a fire which had been left by some wandering beggars, and was overcome with delight at the warmth I experienced from it. In my joy I thrust my hand into the live embers, but quickly drew it out again with a cry of pain. How strange, I thought, that the same cause should produce such opposite effects!" Mary Shelley, 'Frankenstein' [9]

Where other artists deal with the traffic between singular and multiple images, between the generic and its particular manifestations, Martin Honert is concerned with the unique as archetype. For him, generally applicable observations can only be made through citing specific instances. Honert shares many characteristics with his Düsseldorf contemporary Katharina Fritsch, among which are their painstaking devotion to capturing the essence of a single object, including an obsessive attention to the detail of production, their use of artificial materials and the typically machine – rather than hand-finished appearance of their work. But where Fritsch will focus in on an archetypal image – whether the Madonna or a rat – and replicate it to form a sculptural installation, it's hard to imagine Honert ever wishing to repeat a single image unless duality or multiplicity were themselves part of the object's nature, as in the reflection/mirage image described earlier.

The aura, or psychological charge, of an object or event is not intrinsic to the thing itself but depends upon how often and how significantly it has been perceived by others. Memory, then, is crucial to establishing the specific presence of an object, but in giving it form, Honert relies not on generalised or universal memory but, on the contrary, memory that is tangible in its individuality. This holds true even for the large narrative mises-en-scène which are an important part of this artist's work. His first, 'The Children's Crusade', is a life-sized plastic relief sculpture, completed in 1988 after three years of production. The idea for the work arose when Honert re-encountered, for the first time in many years, the German phrase 'Kinderkreuzzug', and recalled with absolute clarity the strong image it had provoked when he had first heard it as a schoolboy. In the intervening years he had not forgotten or expunged the memory but, so to speak, planted and let it germinate. As Boris Groys has written in relation to an even more strongly theatrical work, the multi-figure and many-layered 'A Model Scenario of the Flying Classroom', shown at the German Pavilion in the Venice Biennale 1995, 'The artist does not investigate hidden, forgotten memories that are meant to reveal repressed reality but rather memories that remain stable, constant, unaltered over the years and that resist the power of forgetting.' [10]

The difficult job for Honert lies not in finding an image but in finding the appropriate means to realise it as a concrete object that can be shared by others. While the starting points of the two works already mentioned were childhood memories perfectly preserved, photographs often provide the foundation for the realisation of experience as a sculptural object. This is nowhere more clearly conveyed than in the work actually entitled 'Foto', 1993. A boy sits small and alone at a full-size kitchen table. The image is in fact derived from a photograph of Honert as a child, flanked by his mother and father. For the sculpture he has removed these other figures, to emphasise the young boy's isolation in an adult world. What he has not changed is the physical atmosphere conveyed by the captured memory, since to do so would be to deny its integrity as one particular if small measure of a small human life. The boy's face has been painted so that, whatever the circumstances of the work's installation in a gallery, it will always appear to be lit by strong daylight from its left, the right side of the face darkening into shadow. Acting not just as a representation of the real source image, but as that image itself, the photograph retains its authority here as a specific memorial to a moment.

In 1992 Honert exhibited three separate works together under the single exhibition title 'Brachland', or 'Fallow Land'. Two of these, 'Fire' and 'Bird', are shown here; the third was a reduced model of a railway hut. Together and individually, these three images successfully convey the character of those in-between territories familiar to most of us: the margins just outside a town's boundary, for instance, or the verge of a motorway or a long-vacant lot in a city, where a unique micro-ecology seems to have taken hold. 'Fallow Land' also seems a telling phrase to describe the acts of art-making and exhibiting in general, in its evocation of a free-zone, a territory of contemplation where nothing exists as the result of unambiguous intention, where objects lie strewn about between uses, where the fictions of the more positive world around are left unfinished or broken apart. This is not to say that the works themselves are incomplete or provisional. All of them, on the contrary, are meticulously realised to achieve the most perfect quality of objective, independent existence. The three-dimensional image of 'Bird' was created by painting a polyester cast from a silicon negative formed from an original clay model after an illustration in a birdwatcher's guide book. 'Fire' was made in a similar fashion, but its source was a specially taken photograph rather than a found or remembered image. The fire is 'life-sized' and fully three-dimensional, while the bird is much larger than life and only realised in relief. The room for conjecture and possibility lies in the shift in scale and register between Honert's works when shown together, and in the gap between our experienced reality of the things portrayed and the archetypal form Honert has chosen to give them. The artist himself has referred to the power of this tension, saying that 'Fire has no need of stability, but the inner image of fire demands a stable, frozen sign.'[11]

For all the thought and care Honert invests in his works, and for all their outward simplicity of spirit, their indirectness as art objects and their material coldness has led to accusations of ugliness and kitsch. Jutta Koether, in mock horror, writes about the 'brutality' of Honert's polyester medium and says, perhaps only partly in irony, that 'it is done in such a frightening manner.'[12] Sophisticated as Honert is as an artist, it seems no injustice to him to claim that much of the success of his work derives from its closeness in motivation to what we know as kitsch. Why else, for example, do people make and buy fake log fires, except to have, close to hand where it should be, a convincing image of the primal fire of the hearth?

Stefan Hablützel also works in polyester, out of which he has fashioned a pair of monumental heads, one male, the other female, which hang directly on the wall like marble busts or hunting trophies. They represent specific individuals, but their identity is not important. What counts is the desire to capture the breath or life through depiction, taken to lengths perhaps no more absurd than those which have motivated sculptors of the real from Pygmalion and Bernini to Madame Tussaud and Duane Hanson. Prosthetics, the artificial real, allows the distinct possibility that mankind's age-old dream of recreating itself – invariably a better and less compromised, problematic self – will move out of the realms of art and fiction. Hablützel's faces stare out upon the world they are entering with a look of confident expectation.

TODAY'S MONSTERS

"Ferrix peered into the mirror and shuddered, for he saw there not himself, but a hideous monster, the very spit and image of a paleface, with an aspect as moist as an old spiderweb soaked in the rain, flaccid, drooping, doughy – altogether nauseating. He turned, and his body shook like coagulated agar..."
Stanislaw Lem, The Cyberiad[13]

Thomas Schütte's 'Grosse Geister' statues look like you might imagine the heroic robot Ferrix, Russian science-fiction writer Stanislaw Lem's character who disguises himself as a 'paleface', or human, in the hope of winning the hand of his true love, the Princess Crystal. Like much of the work in this exhibition, if rather more obviously, these twisted monumental figures seem to convey a damaged innocence, the innocence of the monster, poignantly failing to attain an ideal beauty and doomed to be forever reminded of their base materiality.

Since the beginning of the 1980s, Thomas Schütte has developed an extensive and complex body of work, moving nimbly across scale, material, and subject: between the public and the private realms, indoor and outdoor space, abstraction and figuration, the architectonic and the pictorial, humour and gloom, beauty and abject ugliness. He often reprises themes or subjects that he had apparently abandoned. He has shown himself to be a virtuoso player on several levels of reality and representation at once, most notably in his solo exhibition of 1990 in Bern, Eindhoven and Paris, where he created 'Seven Fields', separate elements ranging from pseudo-propagandistic banners to models for artists' houses, from delicate water-colours to a proposed monument for a missing sailor. Man as a social and anti-social being has been present from the start, and to see where today's monsters emerged from, we should briefly consider the progress of the figure through Schütte's earlier work.

Several of Schütte's first exhibited works, among them 'Ship', 'Stage' and 'Box', all included in the major exhibition 'von hier aus' in Düsseldorf in 1981, employed small plastic Star Trek figurines as futuristic participants on grandiose public podia. These representatives of the crowd mutated into small wooden cut-outs, often seen clustering round subsequent monumental installations like the aptly titled 'Waiting for a Wonder' of 1983 or 'Piazza Uno/Due' three years later. While these architecturally-inspired works led Schütte, in the mid to late 1980s, down one path of public sculpture, their monumental aspect also led him to make more evidently commemorative works, focusing more precisely on the figure. These included a sequence based on a proposal for a monument in memory of the heroic navigator Alain Colas, who disappeared at sea in 1978; and, first shown at 'documenta' in 1992, the remarkable group of painted ceramic sculptures entitled 'The Strangers'. A more private, but key, work was 'Mohr's Life' of 1988, which marked the first appearance of diminutive figures with comic/grotesque features modelled in 'fimo', an artificial clay. These highly individual characters, wrapped in folds of cloth and supported on three simple wooden legs, reappeared most significantly in the bound pairs of sculptures called 'United Enemies' and the close-up photographs of these figure's faces, given the title of the 'Innocenti'. Two more related groups complete the general typology of Schütte's figures: first, a significant number of clay or bronze portrait heads, sometimes double-faced, which rest upon the floor; second, a series starting as far back as 1982 with 'Man in the Mud and Dog' (which precisely represented a figure apparently rising out of the mire) and culminated in the 'Respect' series – 'No Respekt', 'Kleiner Respekt' and 'Grosser Respekt' of 1994, in which figures again seemed embedded into or arising out of a pool made of the same bronze as themselves, surrounded but largely ignored by small cursorily-formed figurines.

In 1995 and 1996, many aspects of this evident fascination with the figure appear to have come together into a group, which is still growing, of misshapen aluminium statues. These first appeared small, as shown in 'Them and Us', a collaboration with Richard Deacon at the Lisson Gallery in 1995 where they carried round strange hairy pod-like forms made by the British sculptor. The 'Grosse Geister' are carefully enlarged versions of the small figures. Although one version has been cast in steel and one in bronze, most, including the three shown here, are made in aluminium both for practical reasons (it is lighter) and because aluminium gives the illusion of being all surface, with very little weight or depth beneath it. It therefore looks more malleable and slippery. The title' Grosse Geister' has a double meaning in German of 'big ghosts' and 'great spirits', generic spooks or luminaries from the past such as, for example, Sir Isaac Newton or Goethe. Their advantage as free-standing upright sculptural figures – remarkably devoid of a determined context, by Schütte's standards – is their freedom of association. They seem to evoke monsters of mythology and of contemporary popular culture, from Godzilla to the infinitely more sophisticated molten killer robot T-1000 in the film 'Terminator 2'. Another less popular but no less terrifying film, 'Tetsuo: Iron Man' by Japanese director Shinya Tsukamoto, conjures up with great energy and visceral power a world where flesh and metal can become one. At the same time, there are in Schütte's lumbering protagonists qualities that refer to a much older tradition, that of the golem, or organic robot, created by the Jewish alchemists to do their bidding, but possessing a tendency to run amok.

Drawing as much on collective memory as the other artists in this exhibition, Schütte demonstrates dramatically, and in a strange way tenderly, that our contemporary condition lies somewhere between the organic and the cybernetic, the self-determined and the pre-programmed, the generated and the invented.

Greg Hilty

References

1. Quoted by Klaus Ottmann, 'Heidegger, Beuys and the Consequences', Flash Art, ... , 1990, pp. 123 – 4

2. Mary Shelley, 'Frankenstein', 1818, paperback edition, Oxford, 1969, p. 221

3. Doreet Levitte Harten, 'We Androids', Artforum, January 1989, p. .....

4. Stanislaw Lem, 'The Cyberiad', 1975, paperback edition, London, 1990, p. 170

5. Neville Wakefield, '"Brasilia": Vanishing Points', Parkett, No. 44, 1995, pp. 78 – 80

6. Shelley, op. cit., p. 57

7. Thomas Ruff interviewed by Philip Pocock, Journal of Contemporary Art, Summer 1993, p. ......

8. Norman Bryson and Trevor Fairbrother, 'Thomas Ruff: Spectacle and Surveillance', Parkett, No. 28, 1991, pp 92 – 96

9. Shelley, op. cit., p. 104

10. Boris Groys, p.20

11. Martin Honert interviewed by Boris Groys, Artforum, February 1995, p. 60

12. Jutta Koether, 'Martin Honert: Johnen, Cologne', Flash Art, October 1988, p. 286

13. Lem, op. cit., p. 286

Plates

Thomas **GRÜNFELD**

Misfit (St Bernhard) *(overleaf)*
1994
taxidermy
60 x 120 x 70 cm

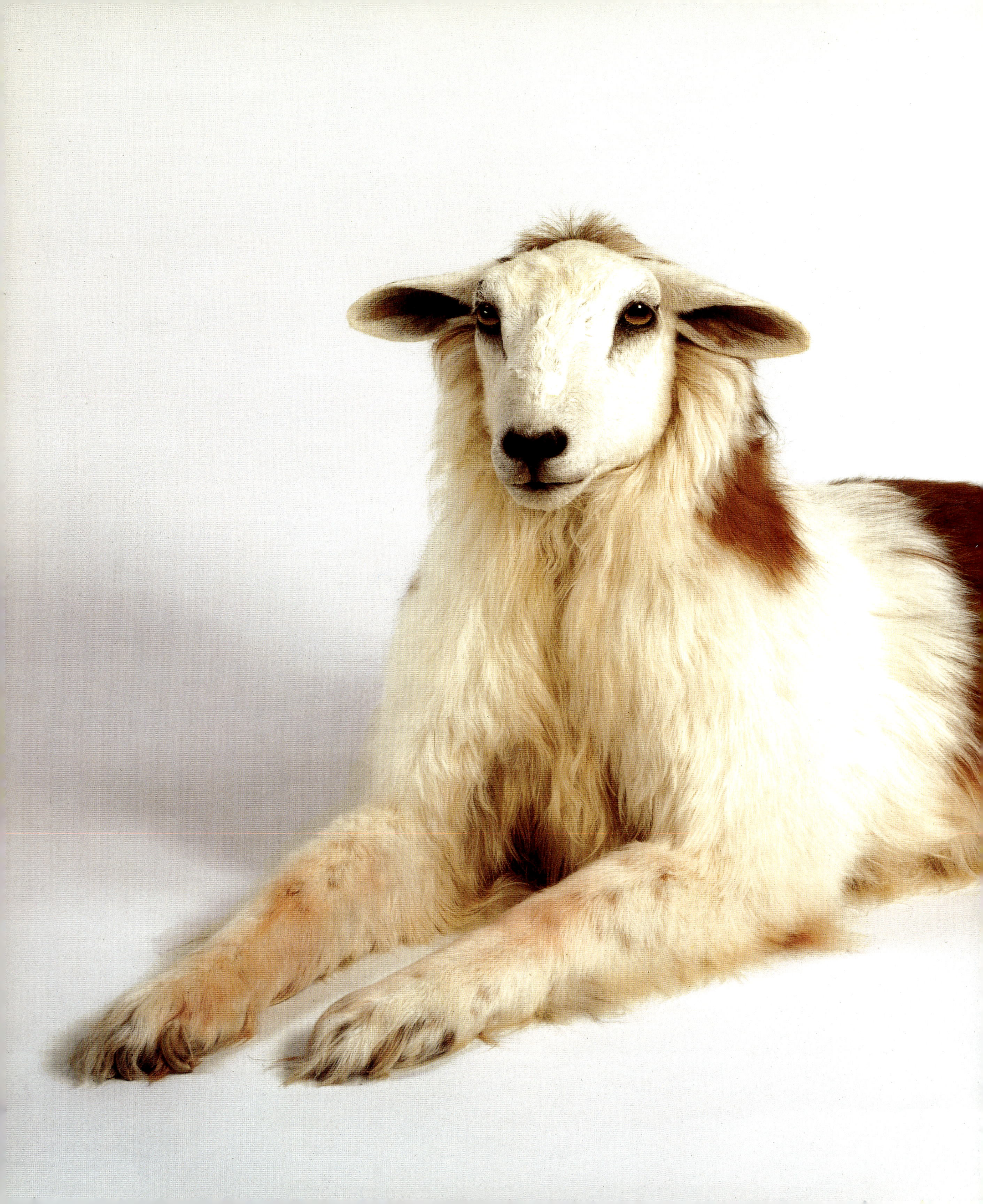

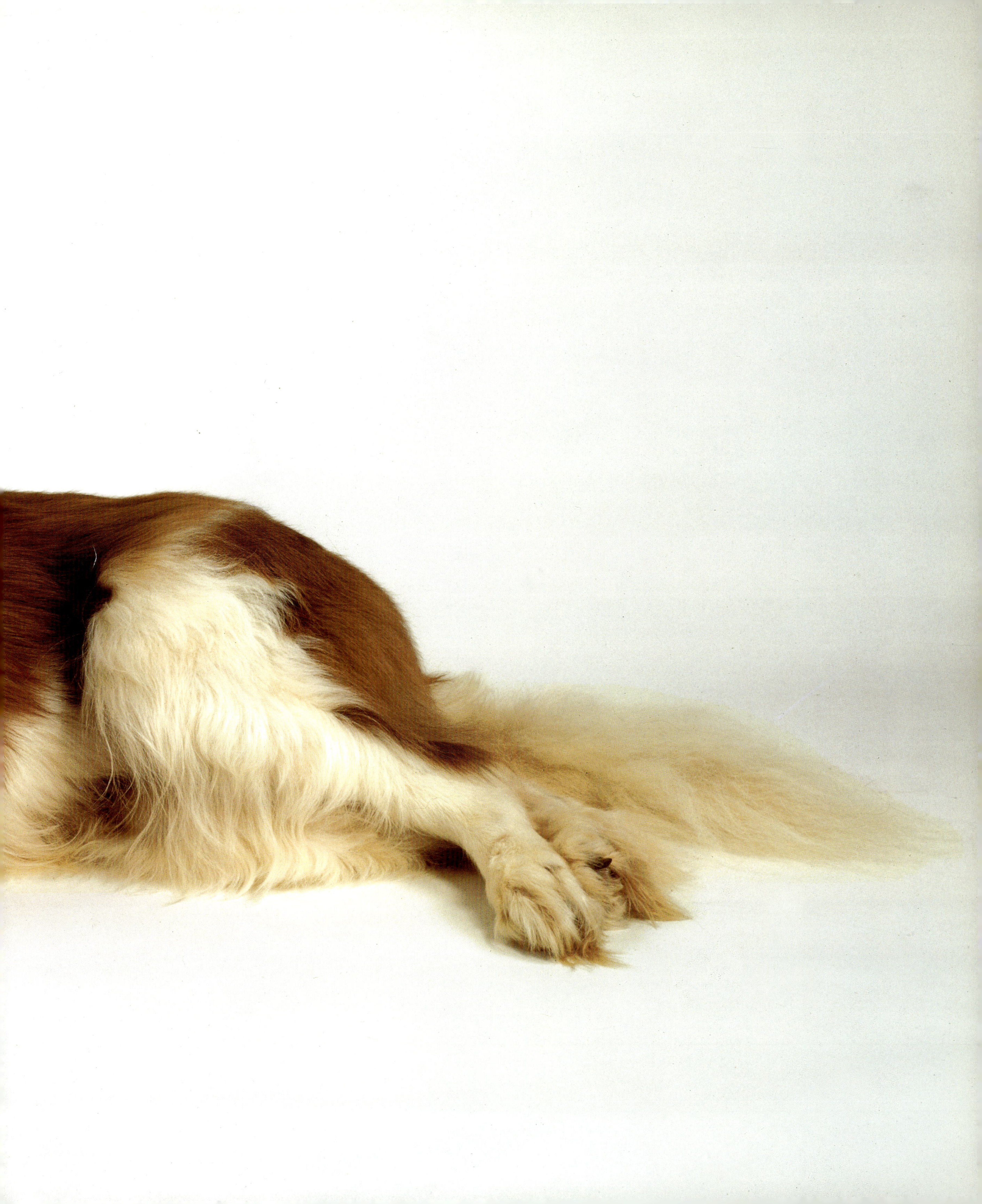

Misfit (Nandu)
1994
taxidermy
120 x 70 x 30 cm

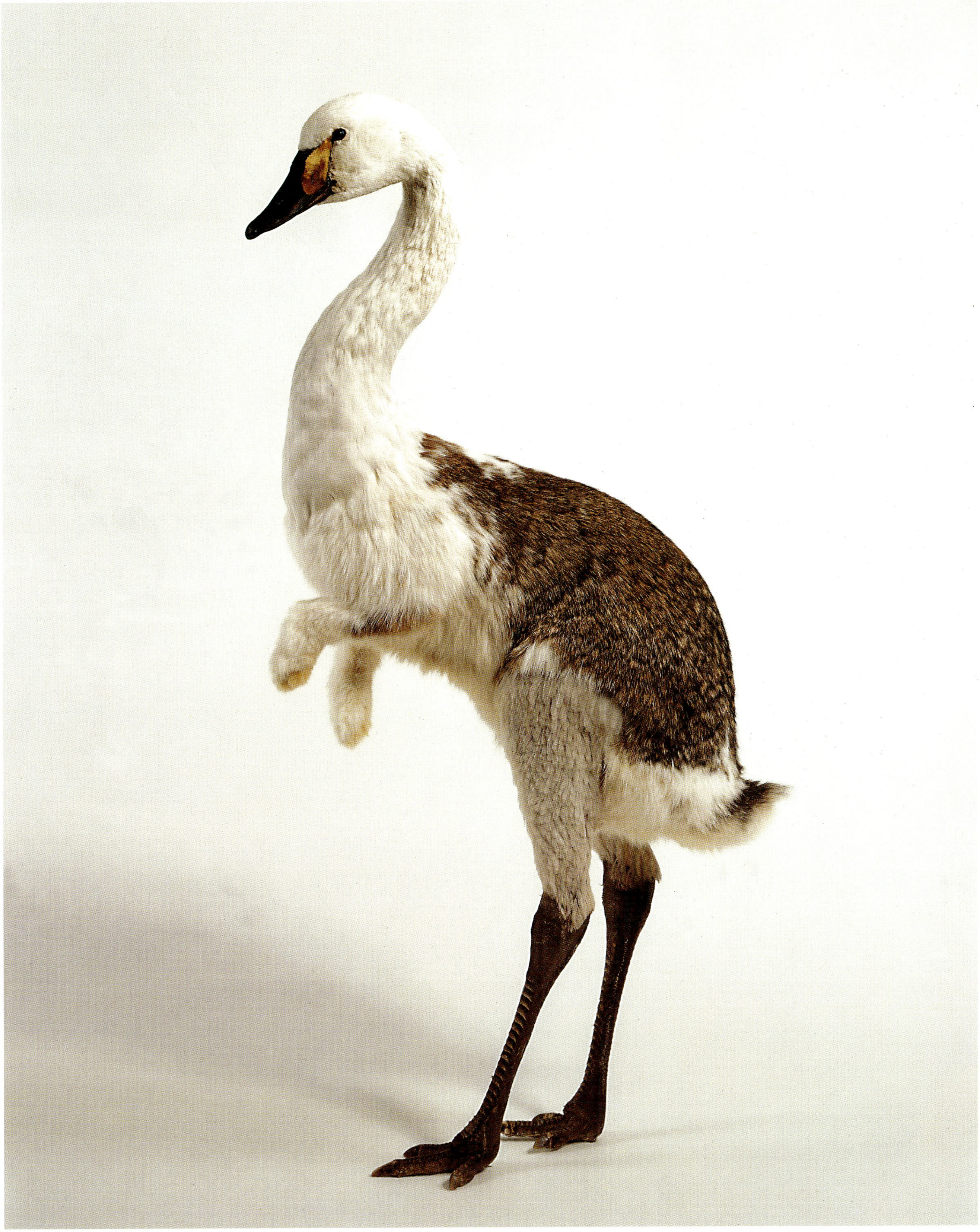

Misfit (Mara)
1994
taxidermy
60 x 70 x 20 cm

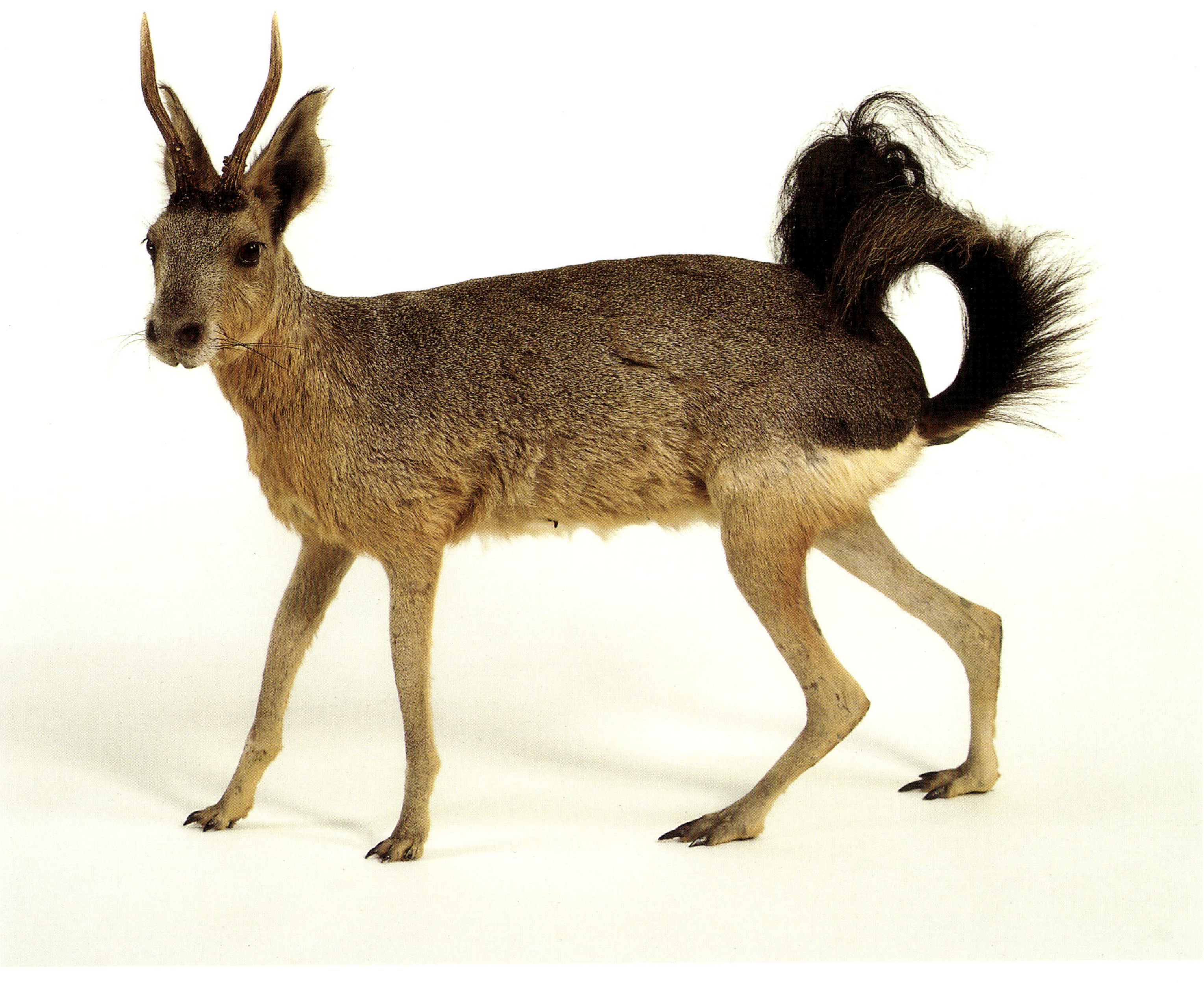

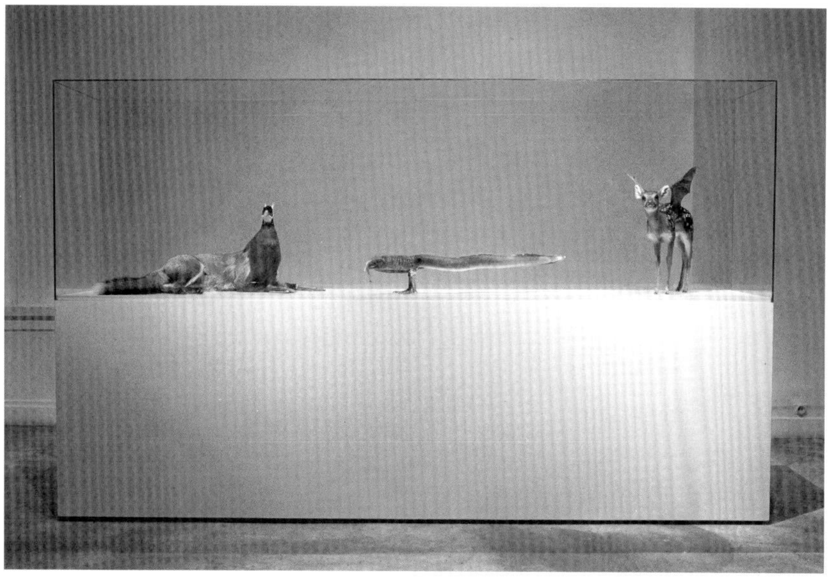

Three Misfits
1994
taxidermy, wood and glass
overall: 160 x 260 x 55 cm

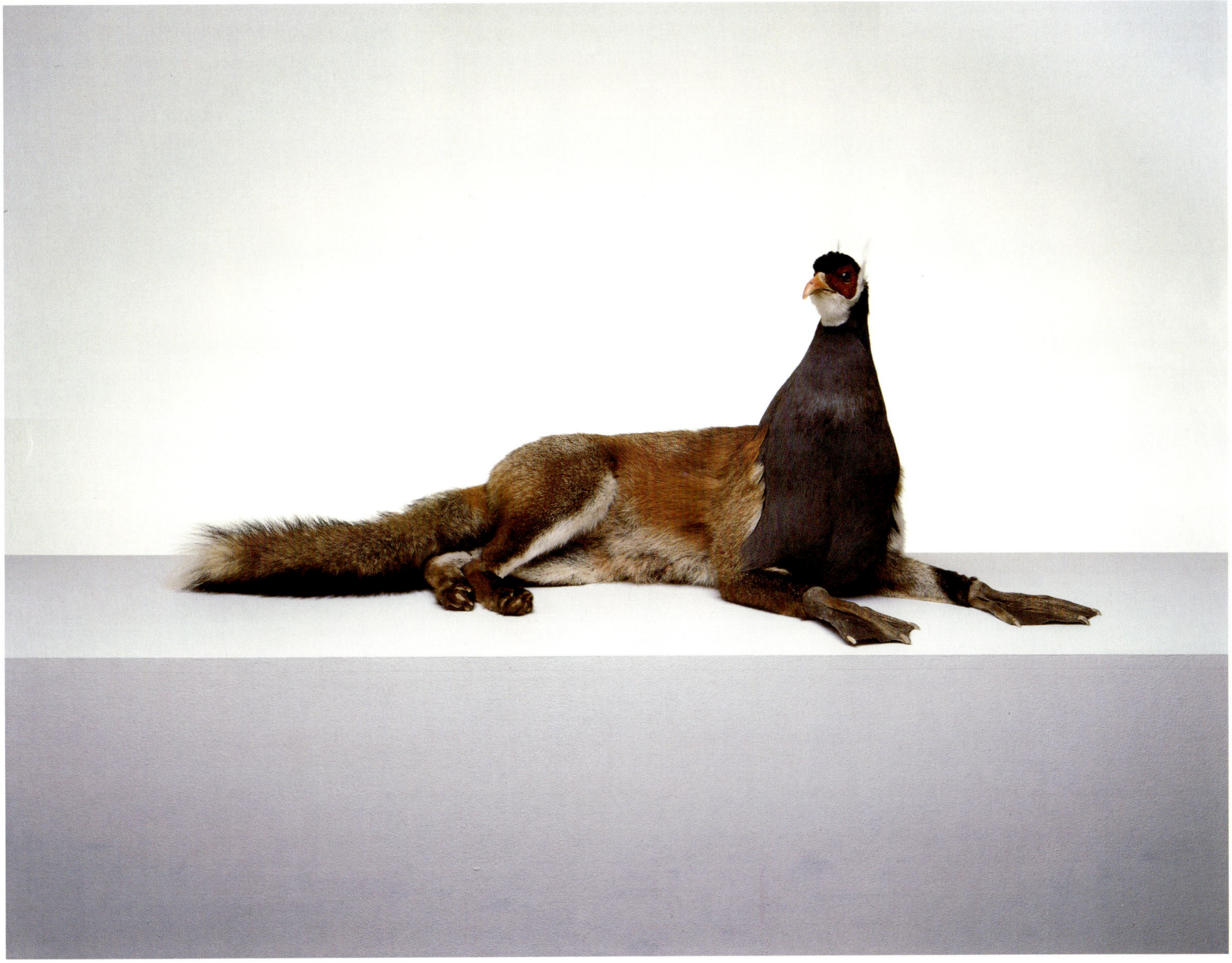

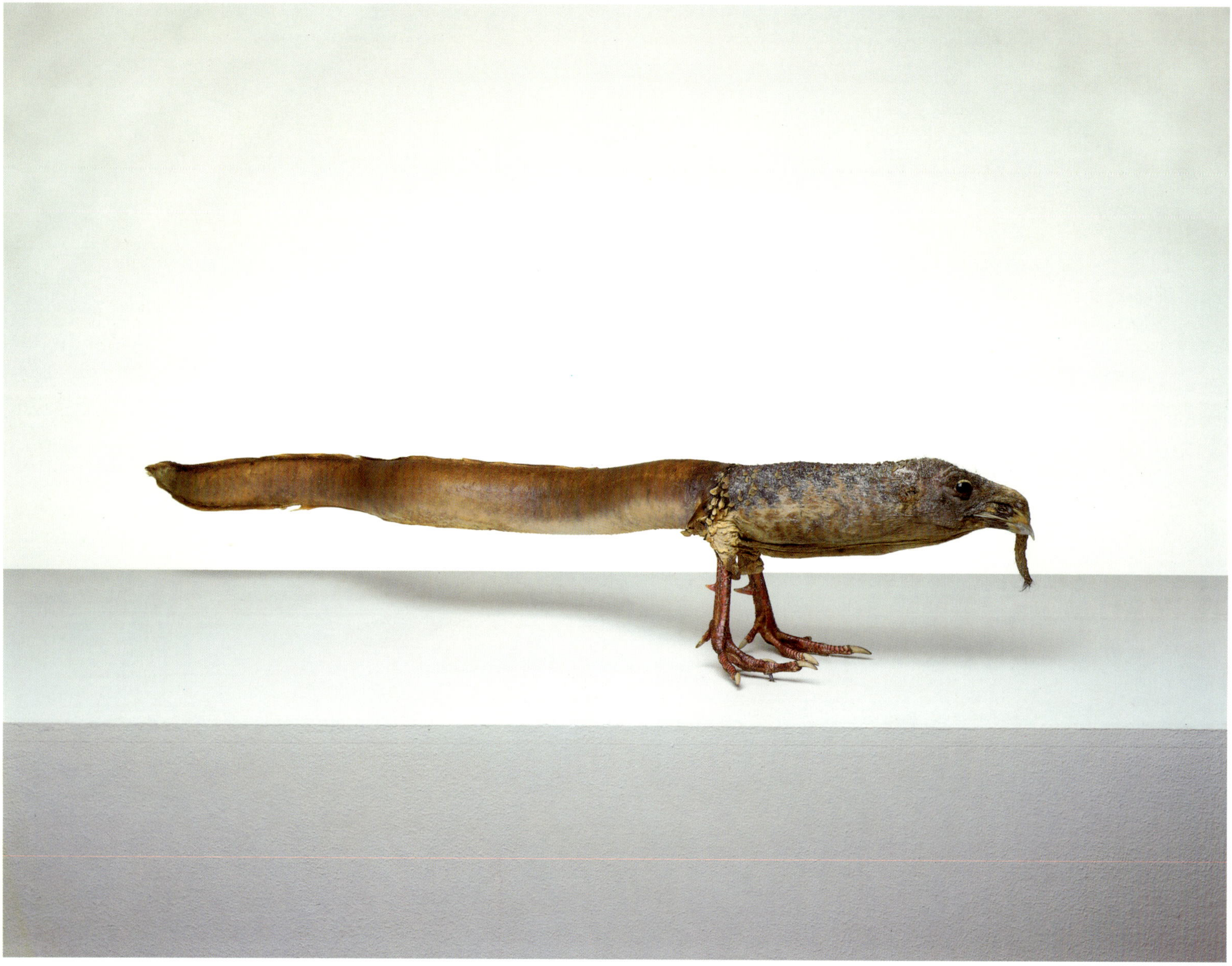

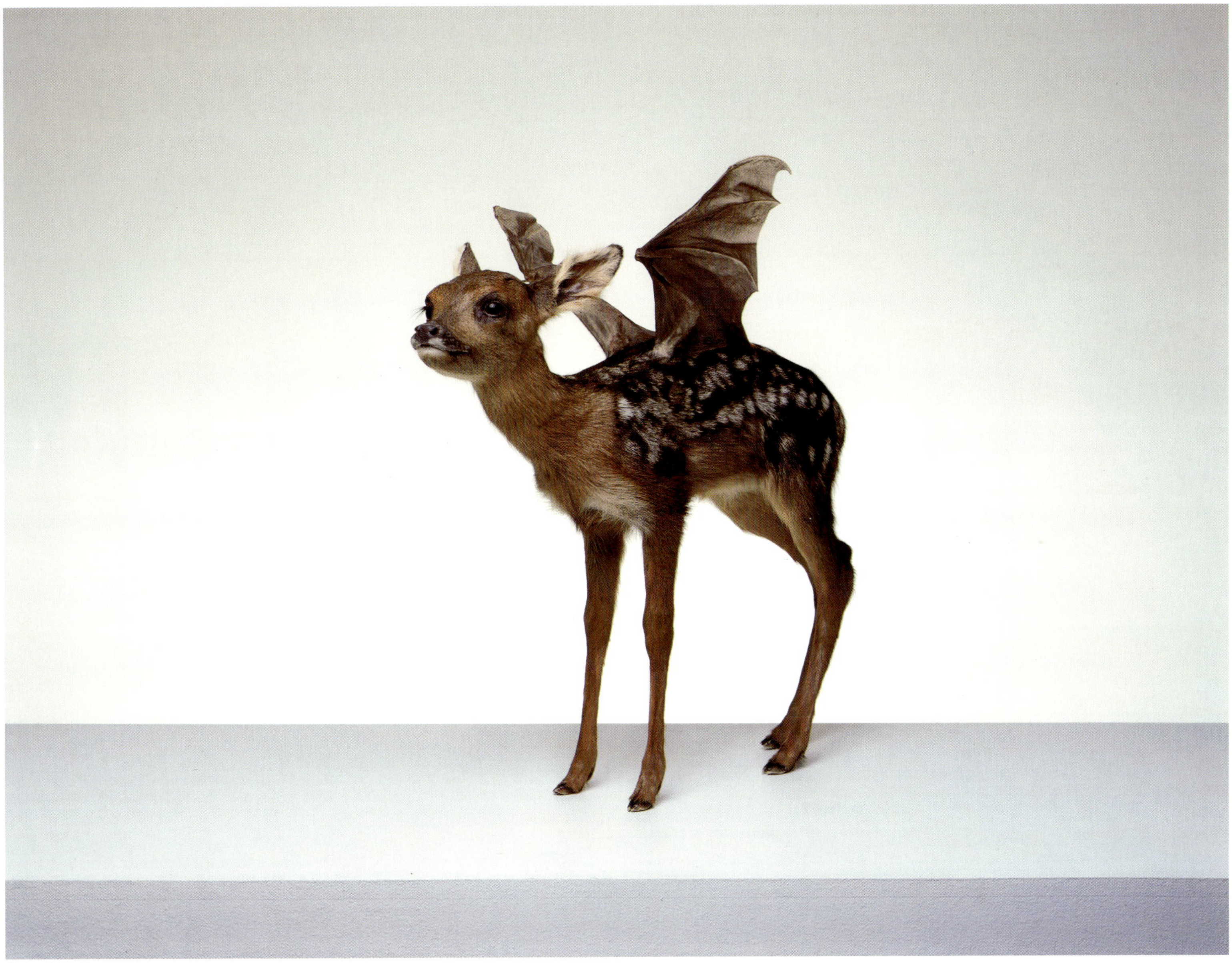

Andreas **GURSKY**

Genoa
1991
c-print
166 x 200 cm

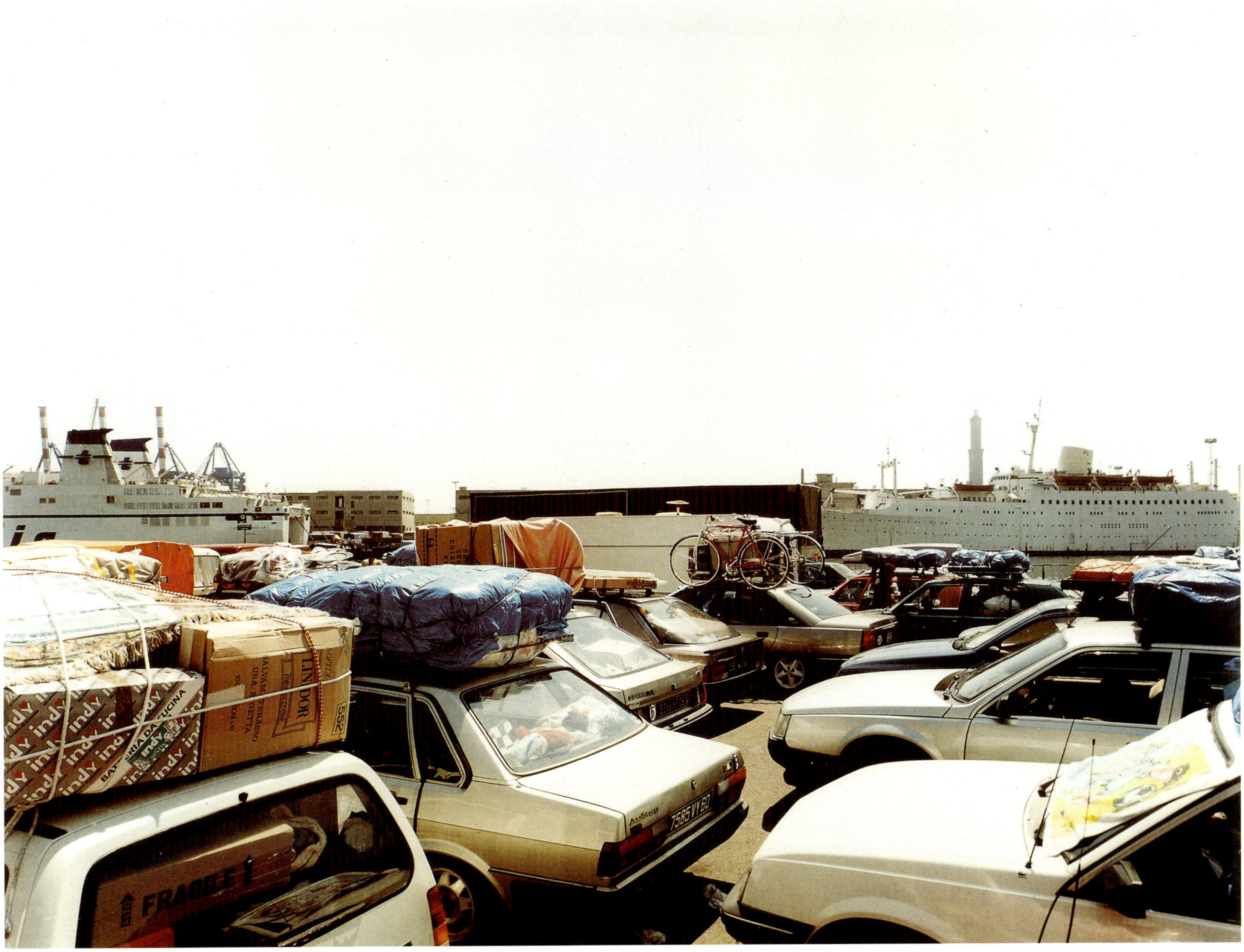
LINDOR
FRAGILE

Untitled 1 (Carpet)
1993
c-print
174.5 x 210 cm

Gründig, Nürnberg
1993
c-print
169 x 204 cm

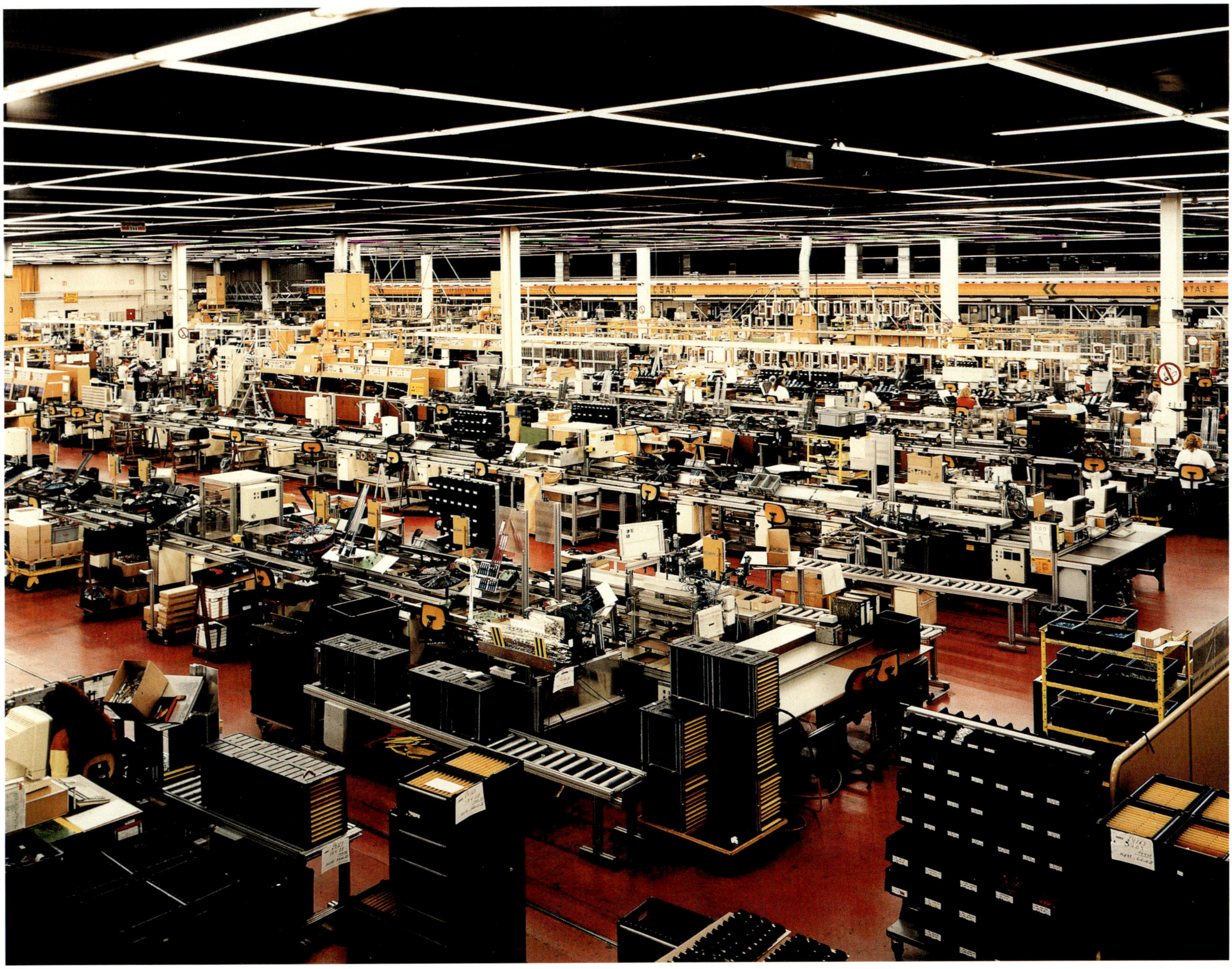

Hong Kong Shanghai Bank
1994
c-print
220 x 170 cm

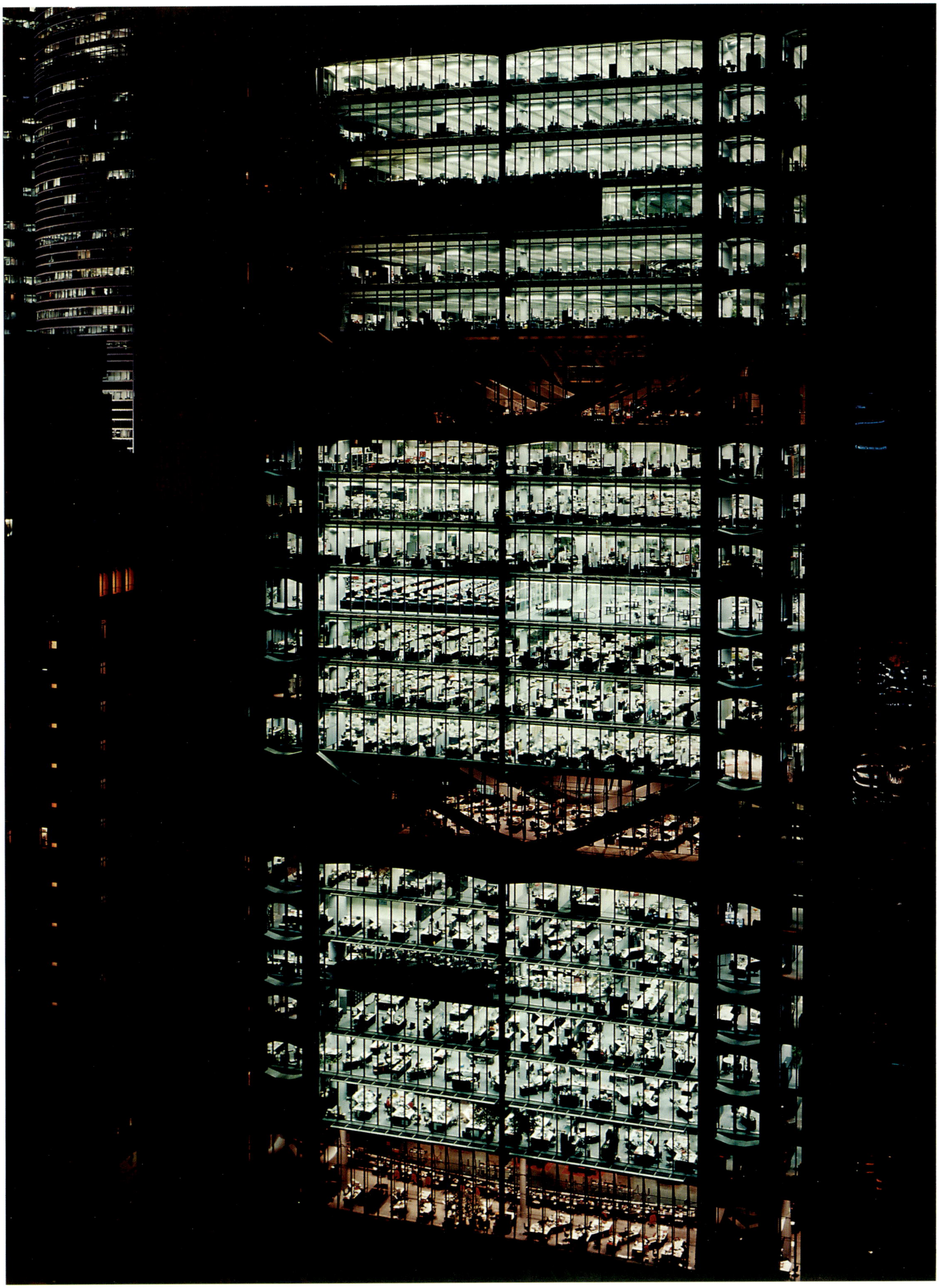

Hong Kong, Grand Hyatt Park
1994
c-print
220 x 170 cm

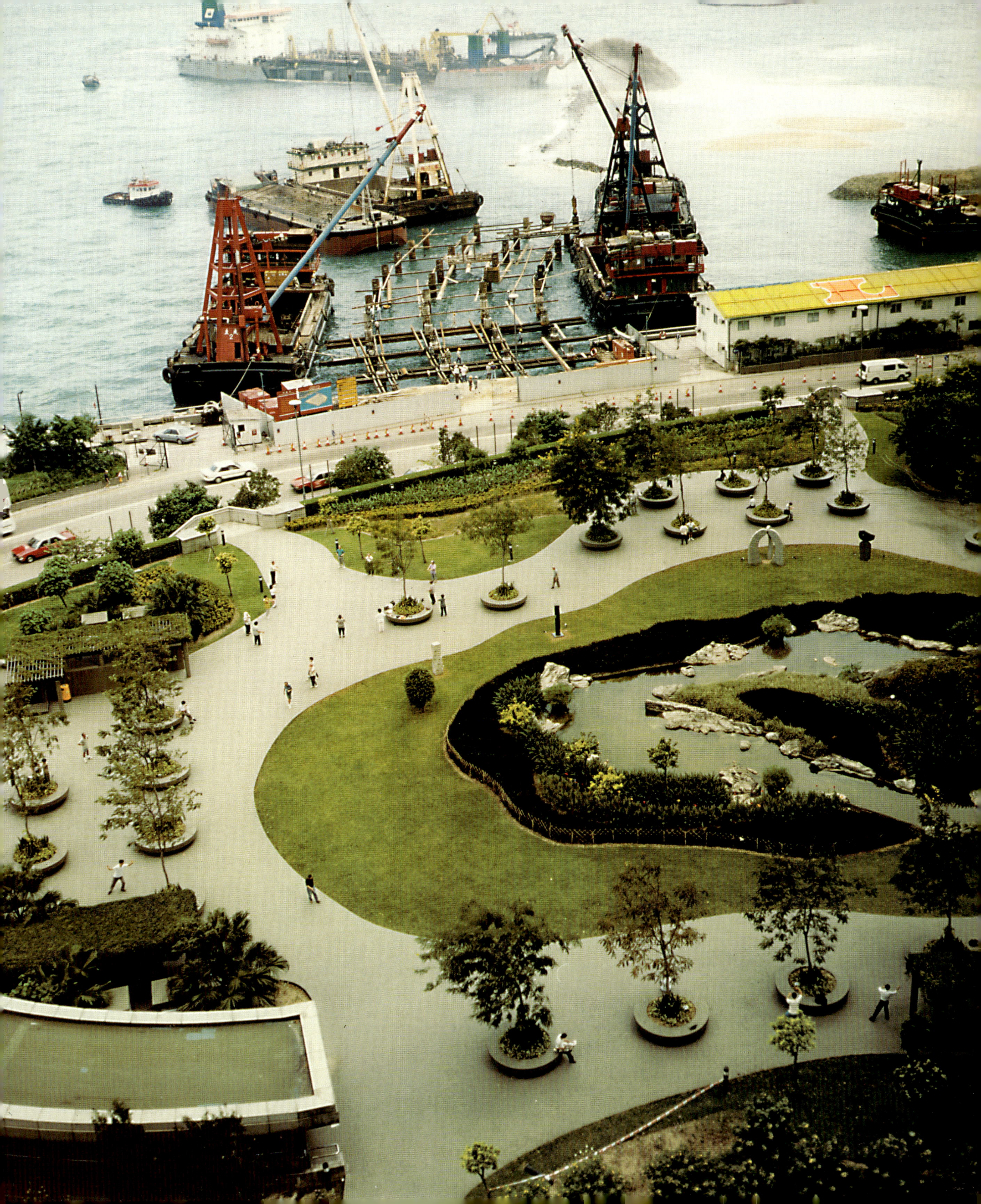

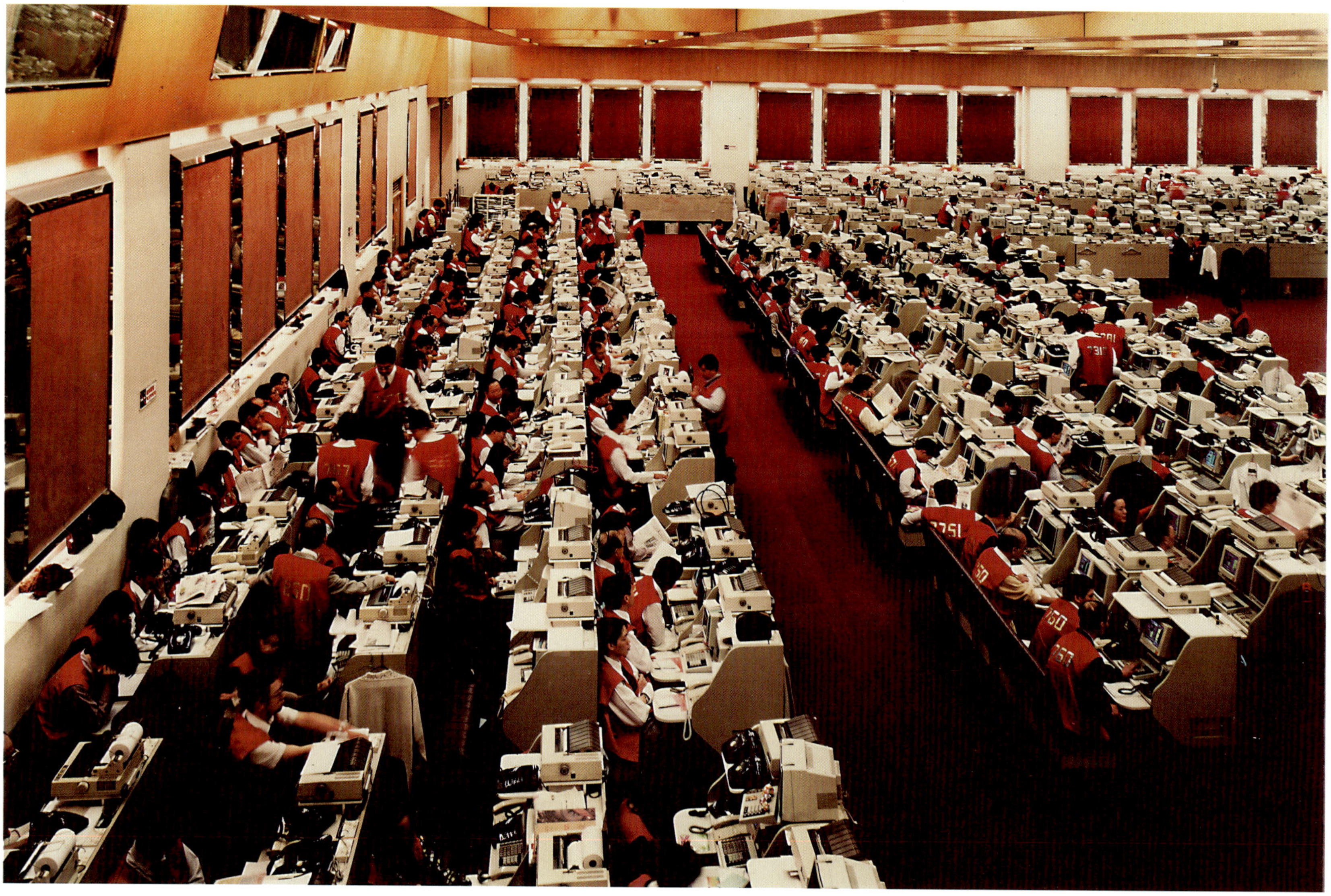

Hong Kong Stock Exchange
1994
c-print
diptych: each 180 x 250 cm

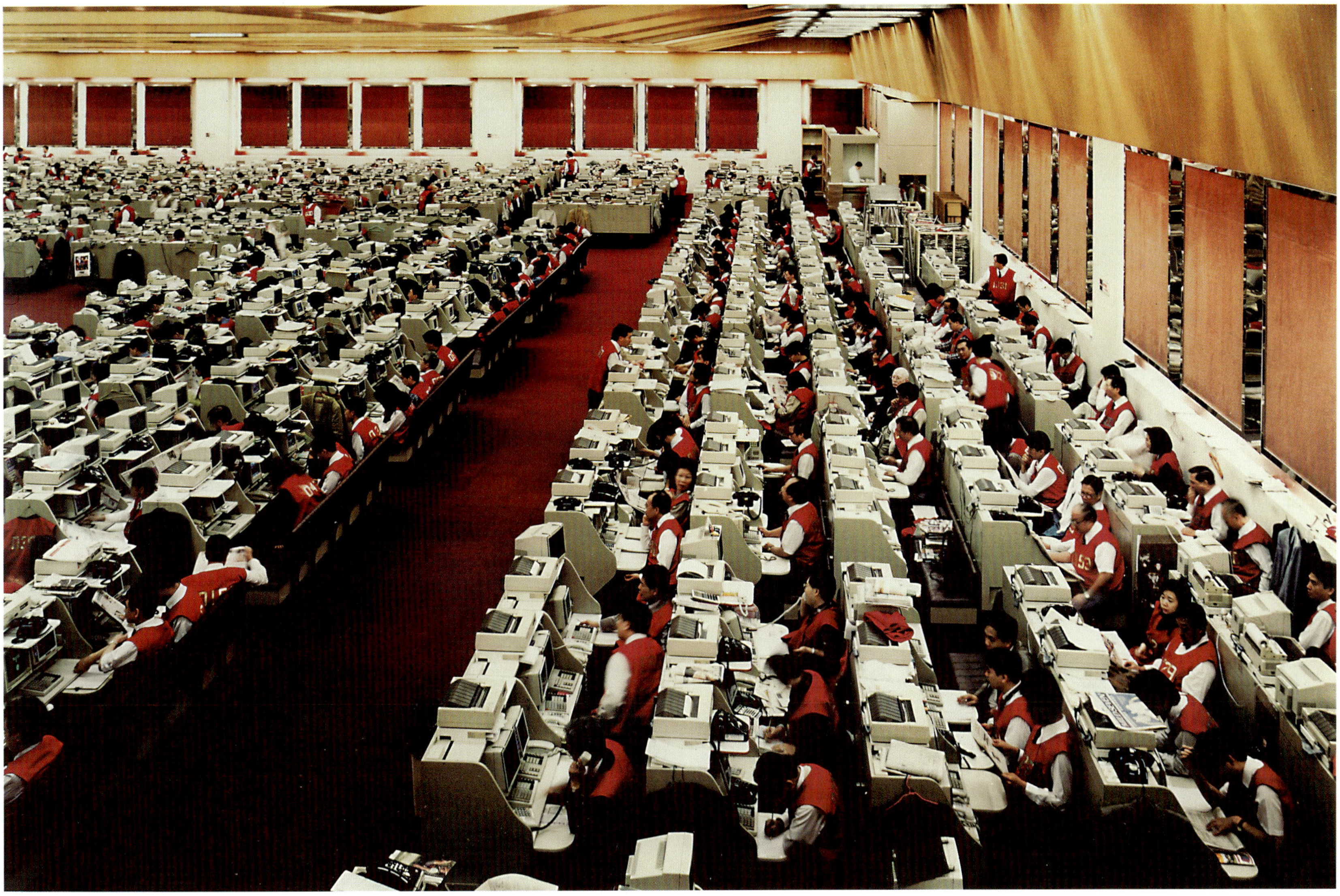

Engadin
1995
c-print
160 x 250 cm

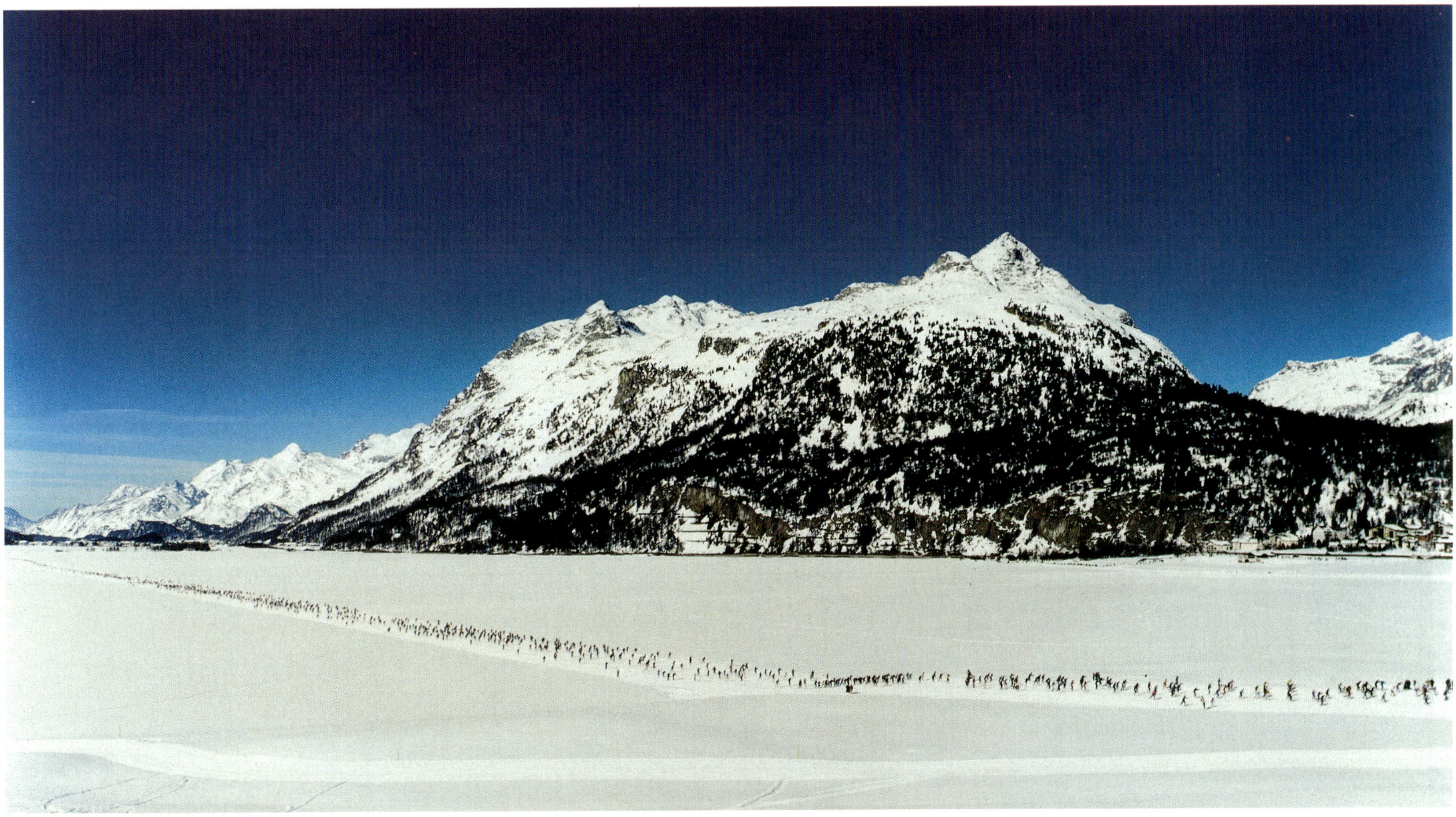

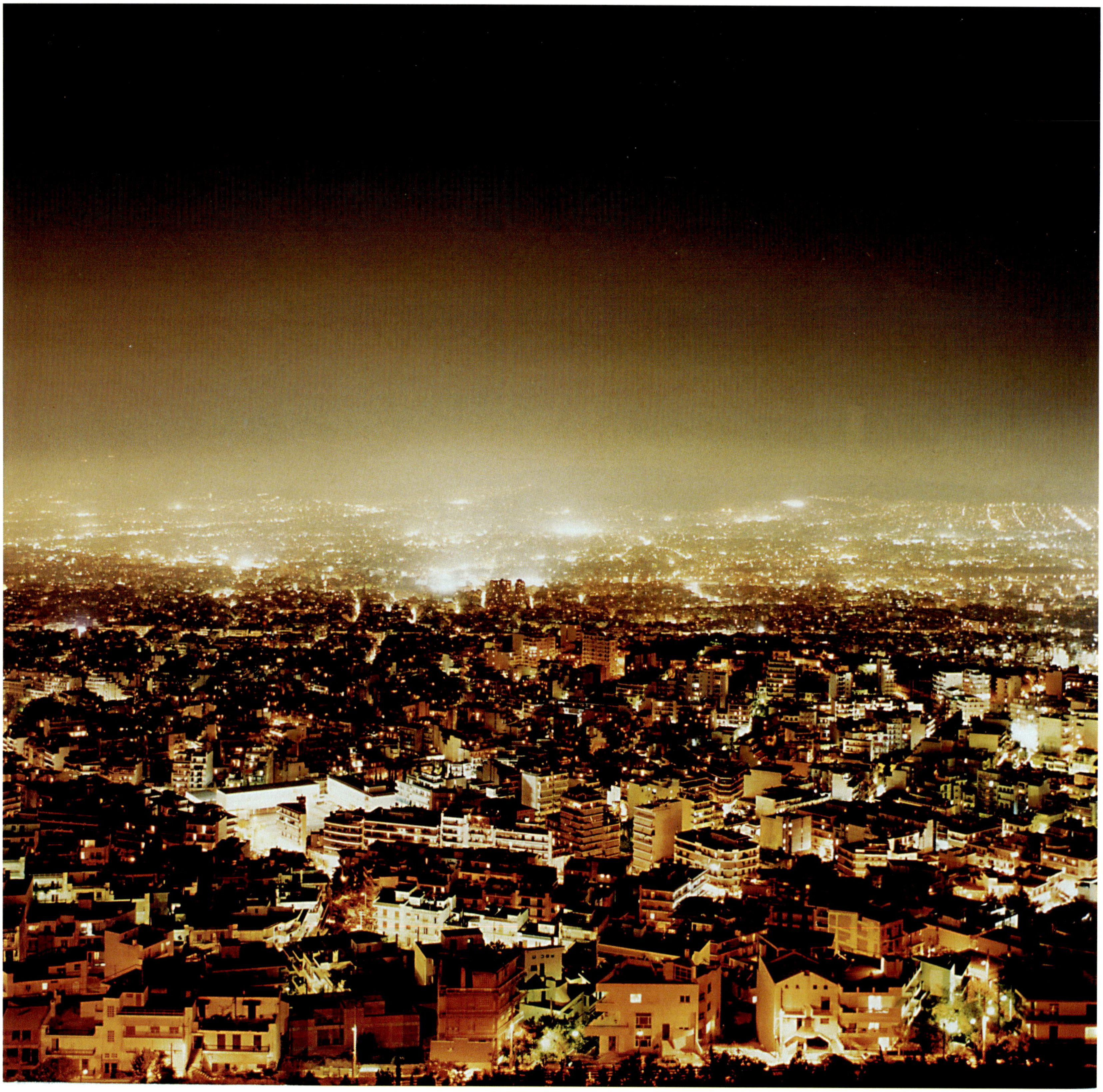

Athens
1995
c-print
each diptych: 180 x 180 cm

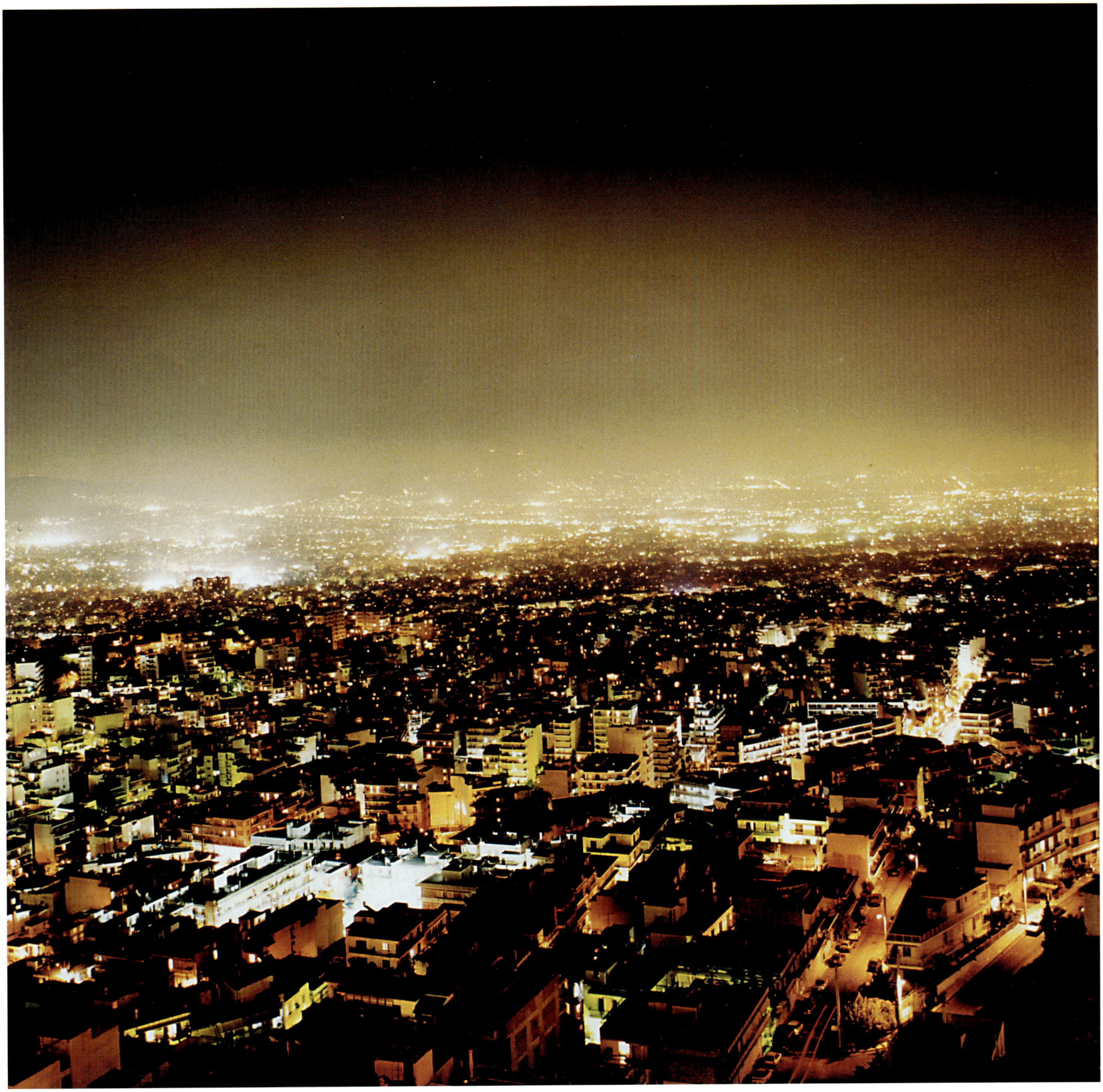

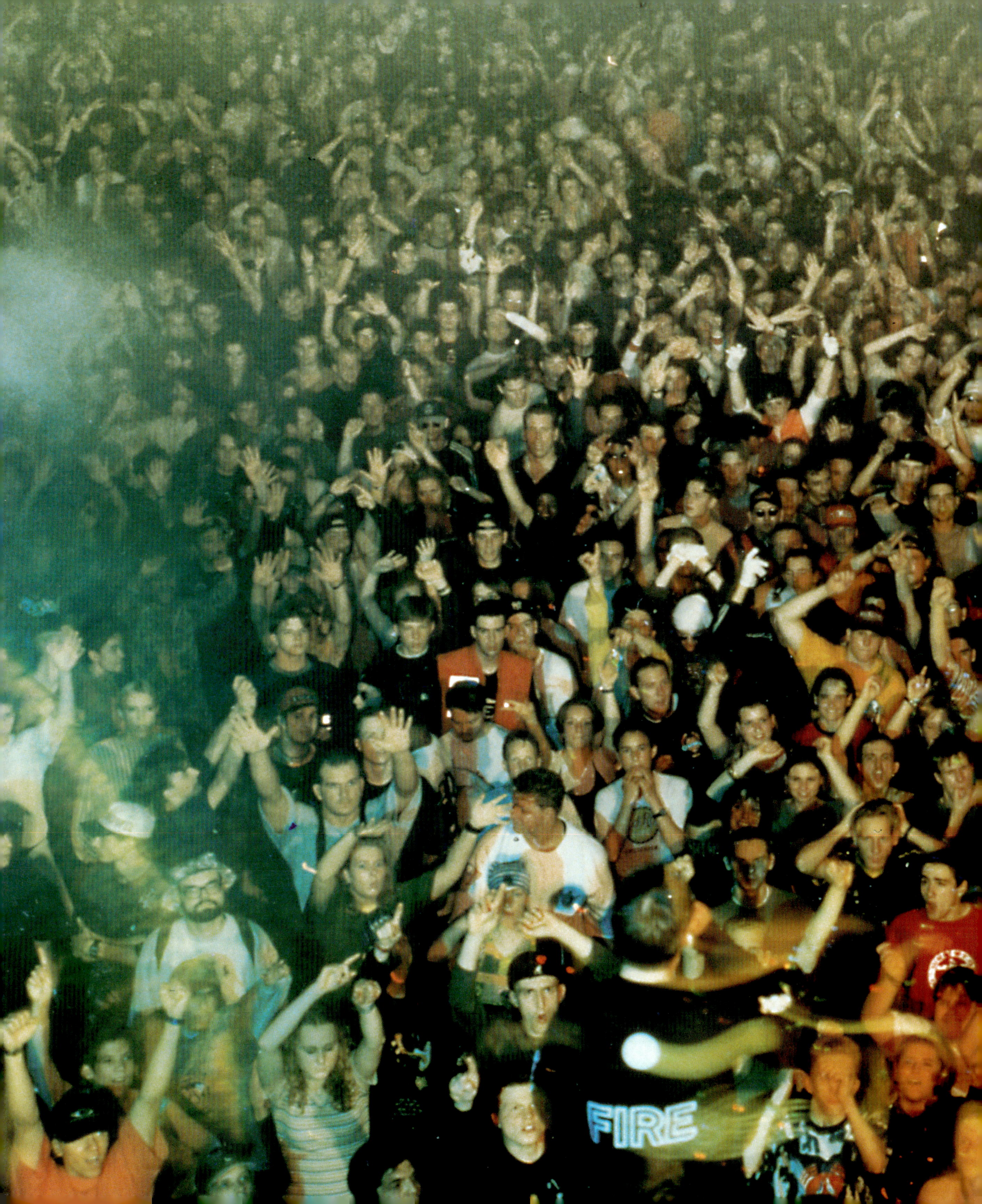
FIRE

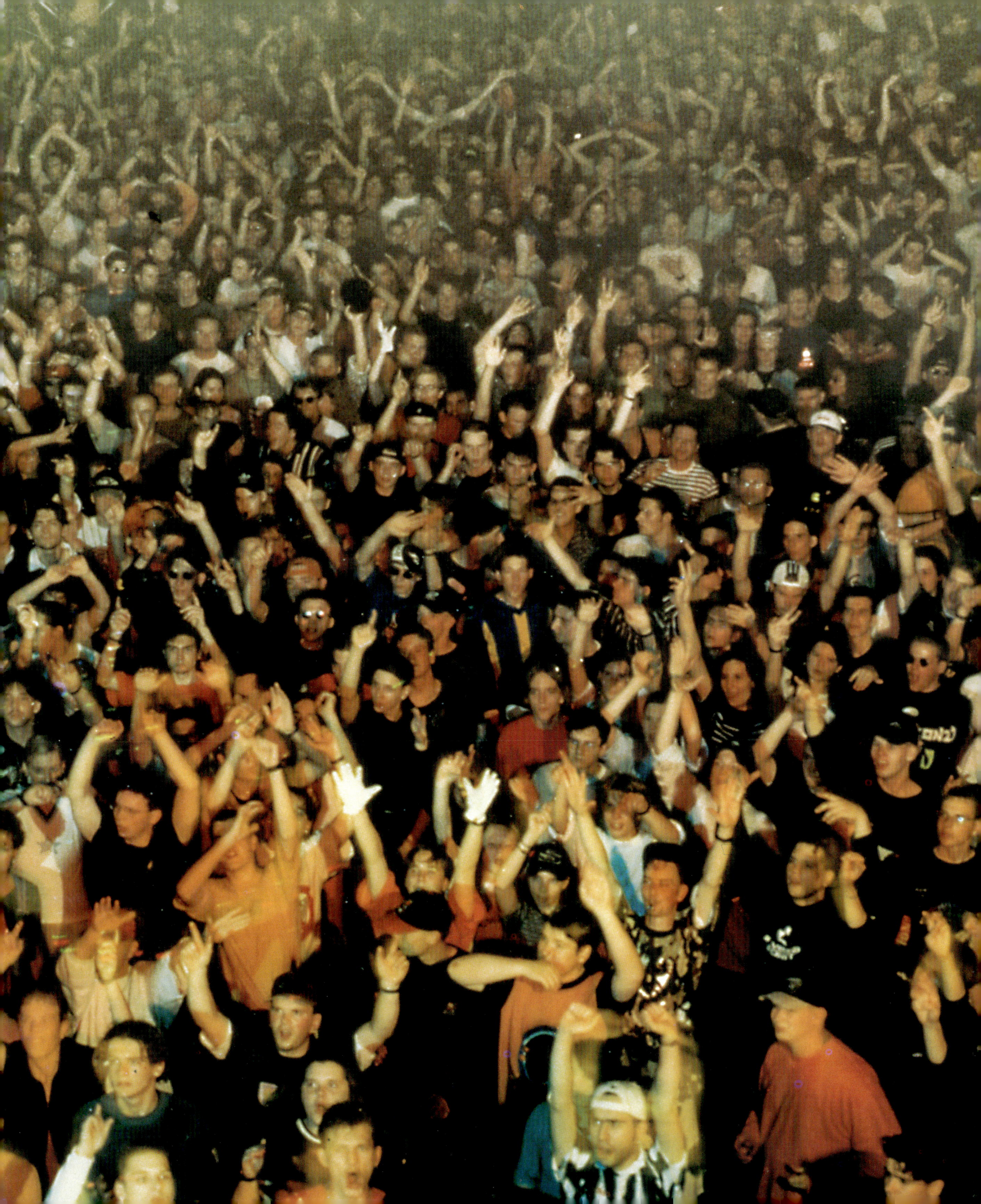

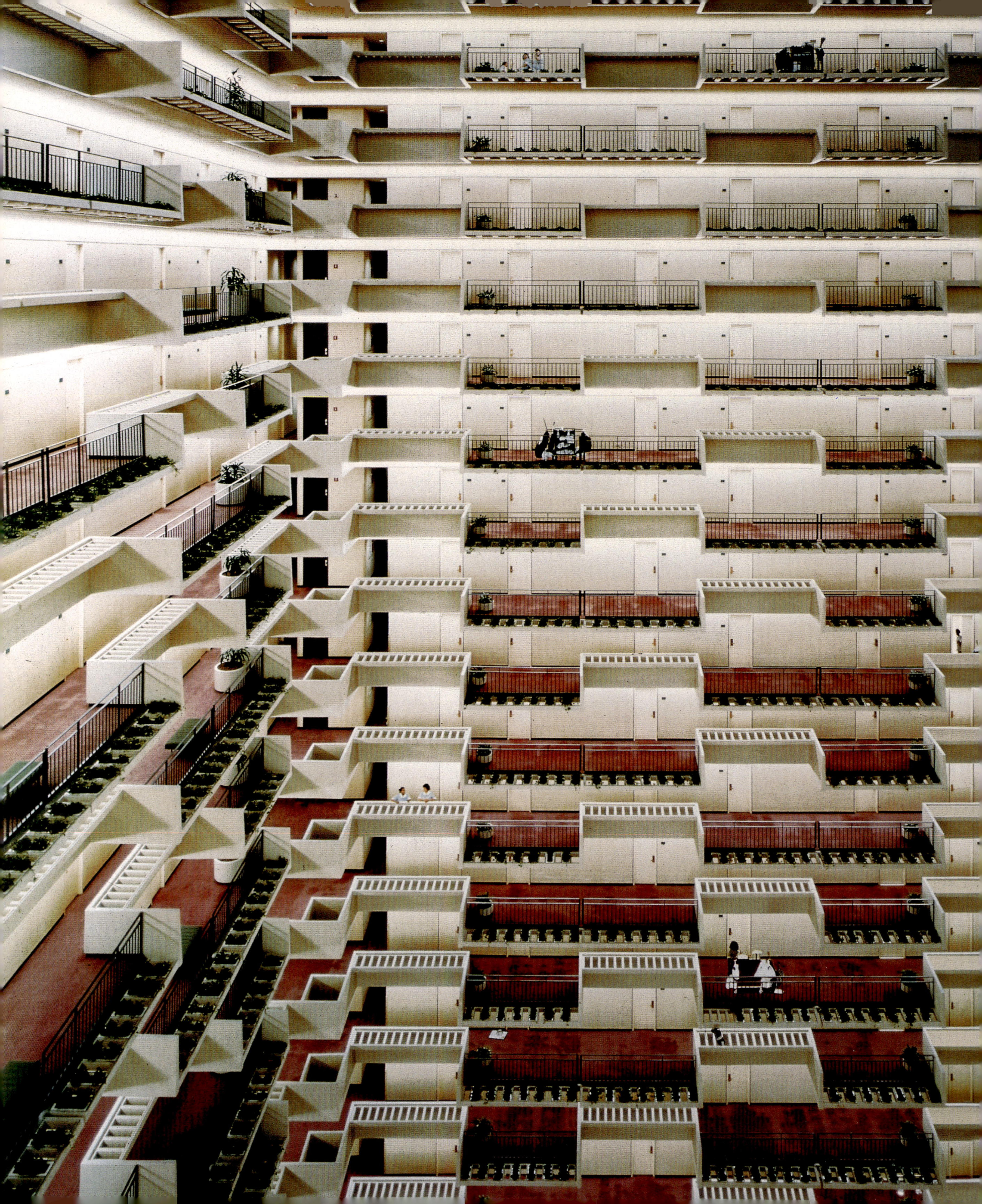

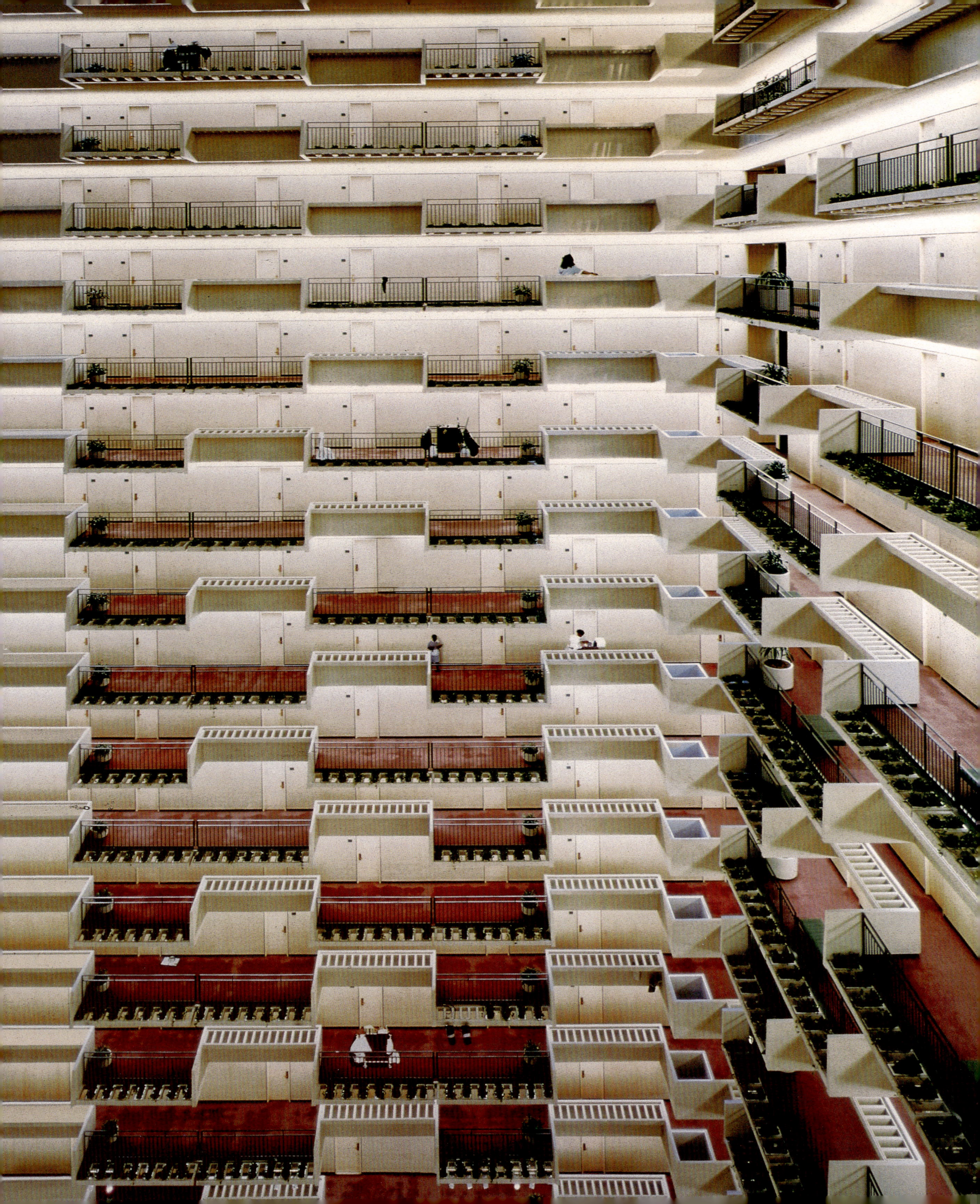

(previous pages)

Union Rave
1995
c-print
164 x 275 cm

Atlanta
1996
c-print
186 x 260 cm

Stefan HABLÜTZEL

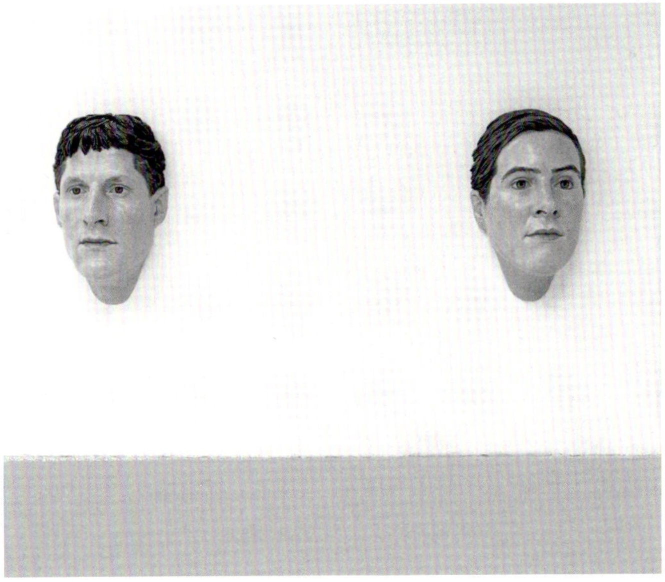

Kopfe
1993/94
polyester, paint
125 x 60 x 70 cm

Kopfe
1993/94
polyester, paint
125 x 60 x 70 cm

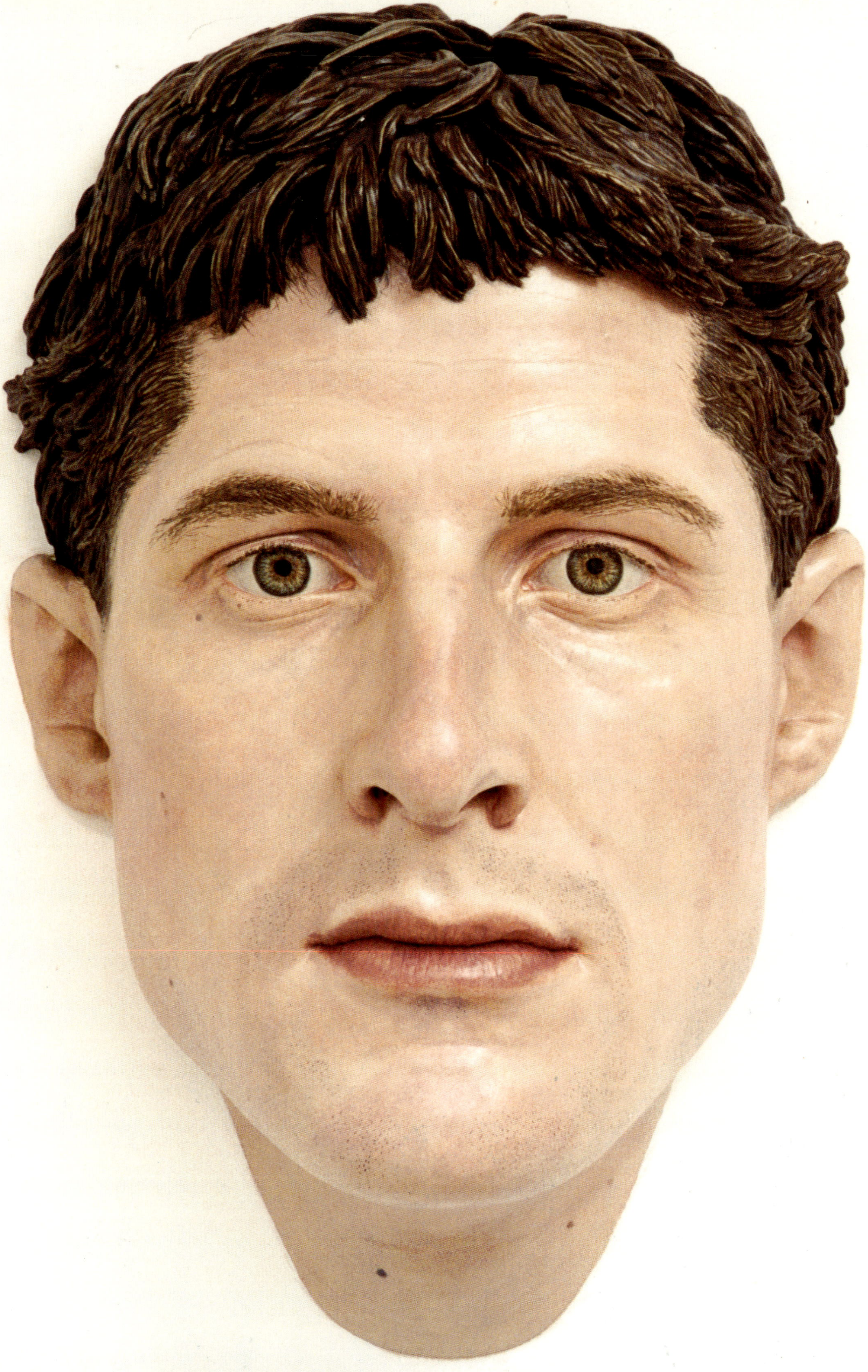

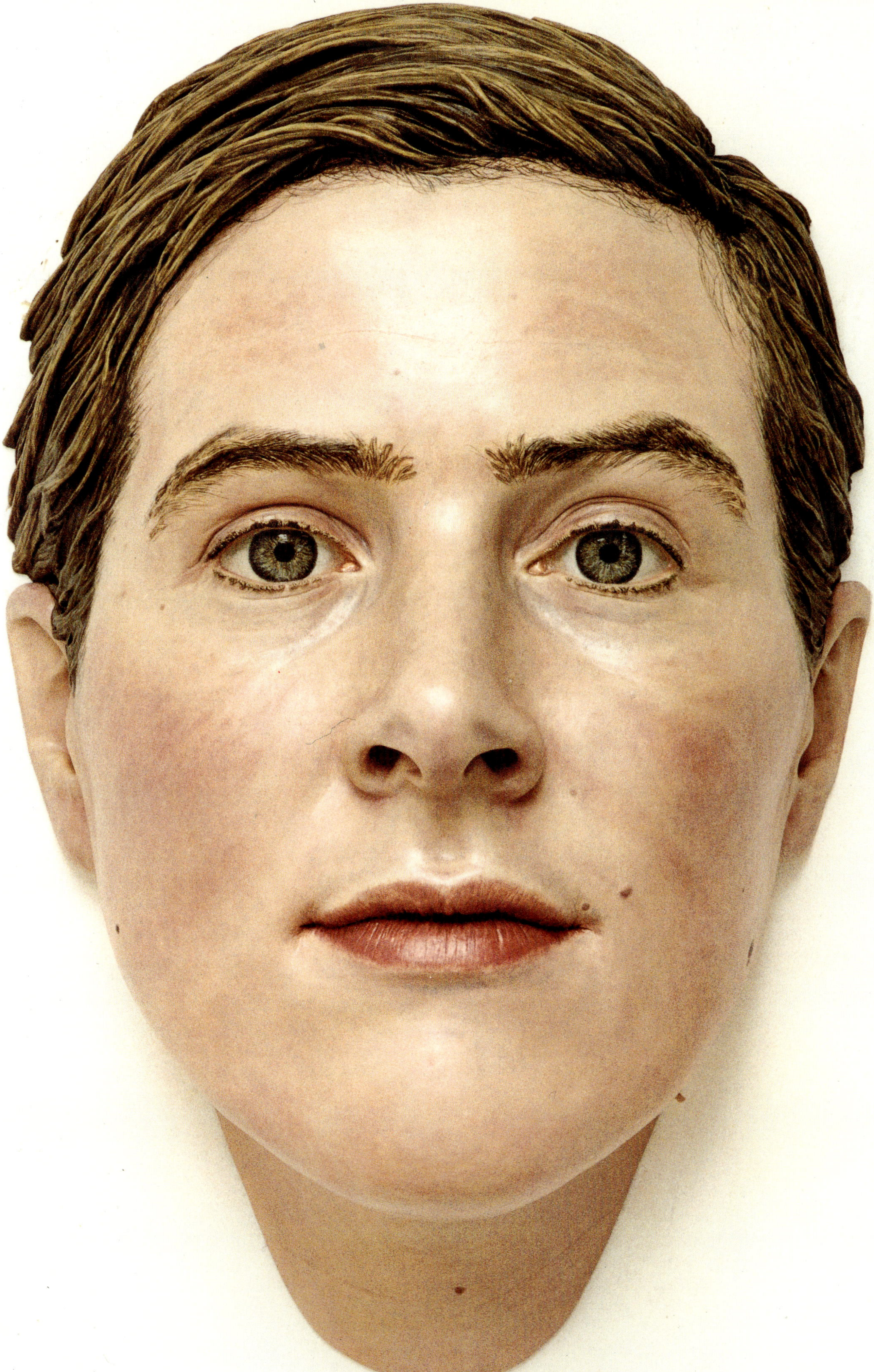

Martin **HONERT**

Feuer
1992
polyester, paint, light
245 x 205 x 205 cm

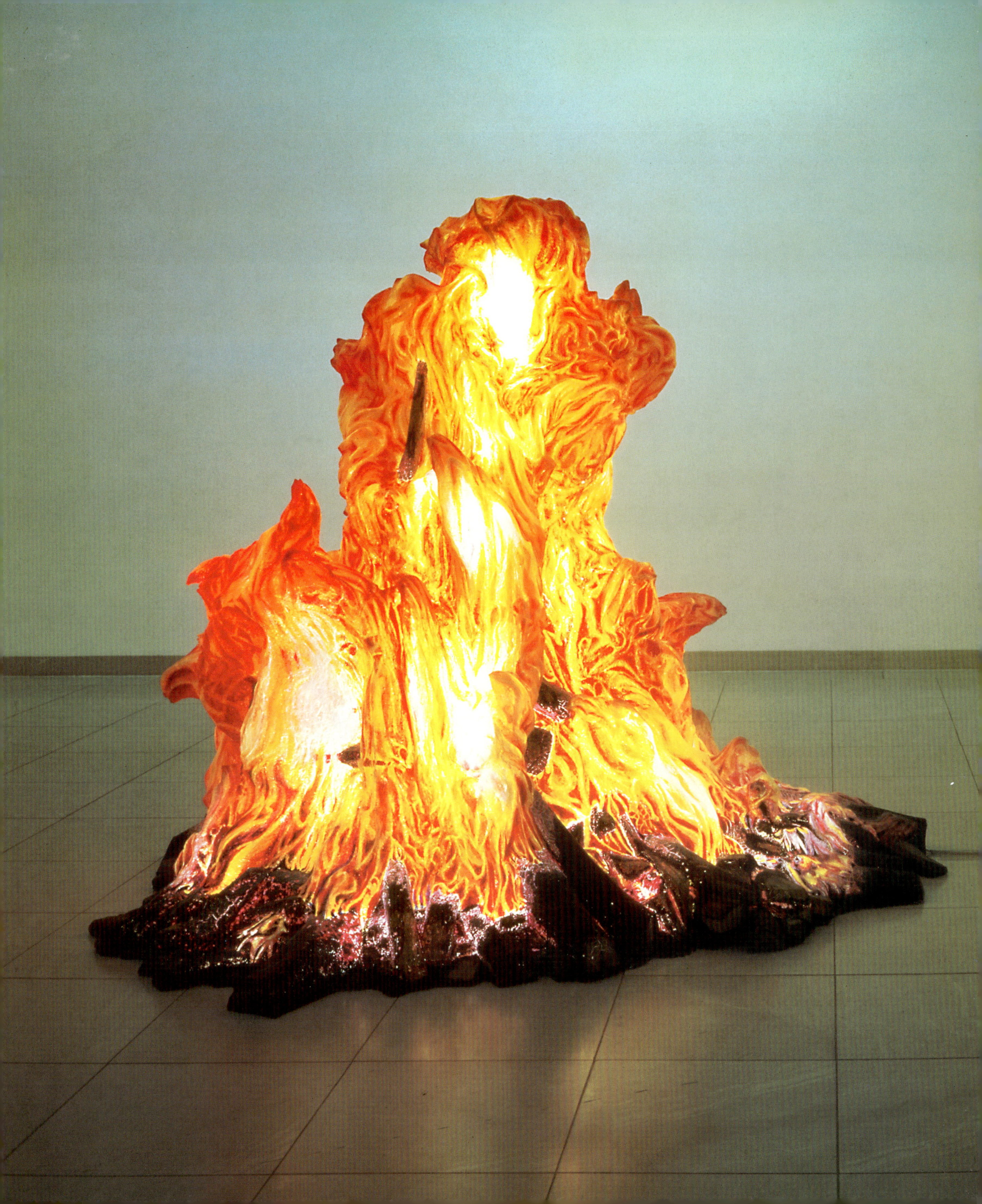

Vogel
1992
polyester, paint
195 x 171 x 16 cm

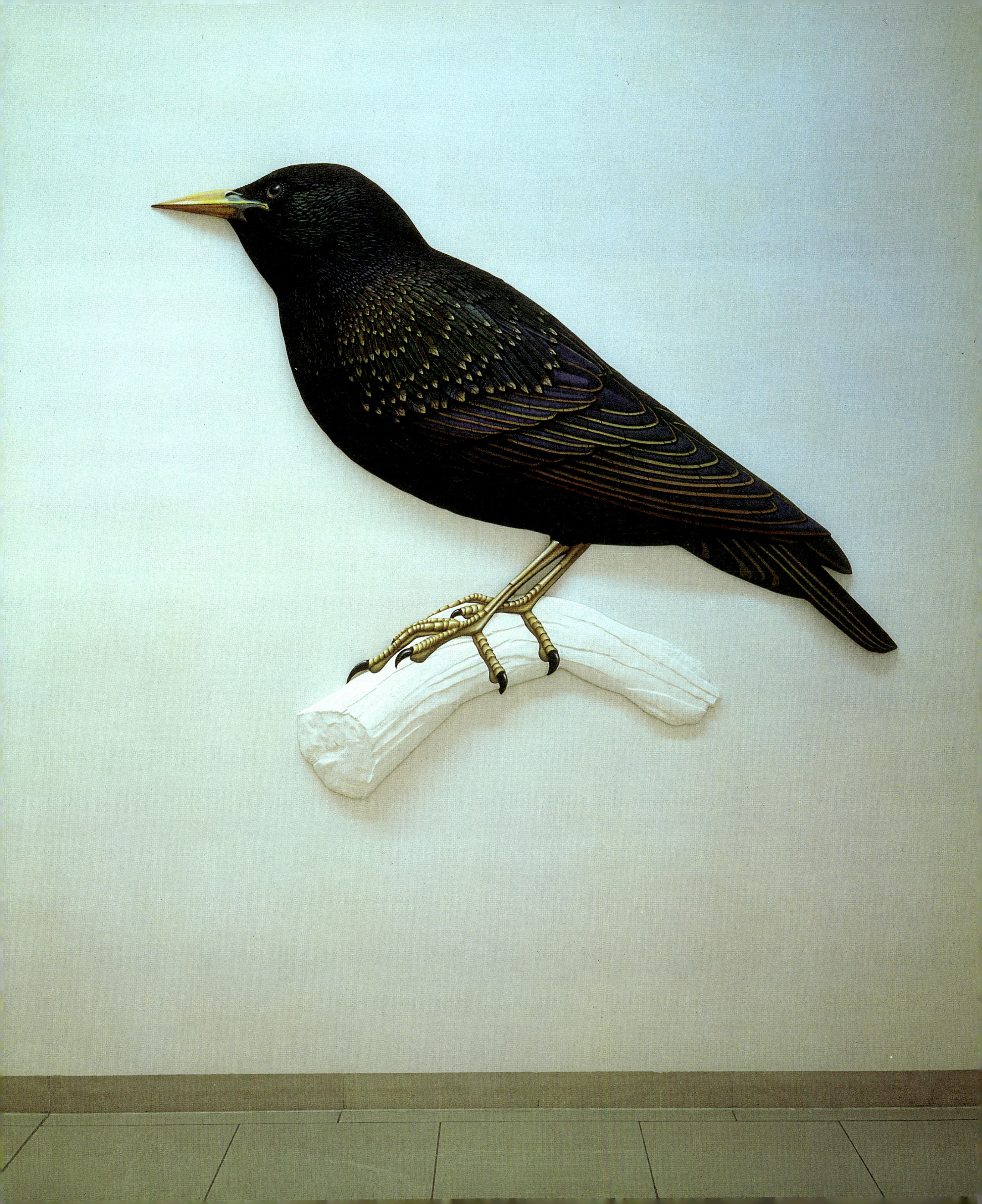

Foto
1993
epoxy, wood, paint
figure: 100 cm high
table: 79 x 73 x 123 cm

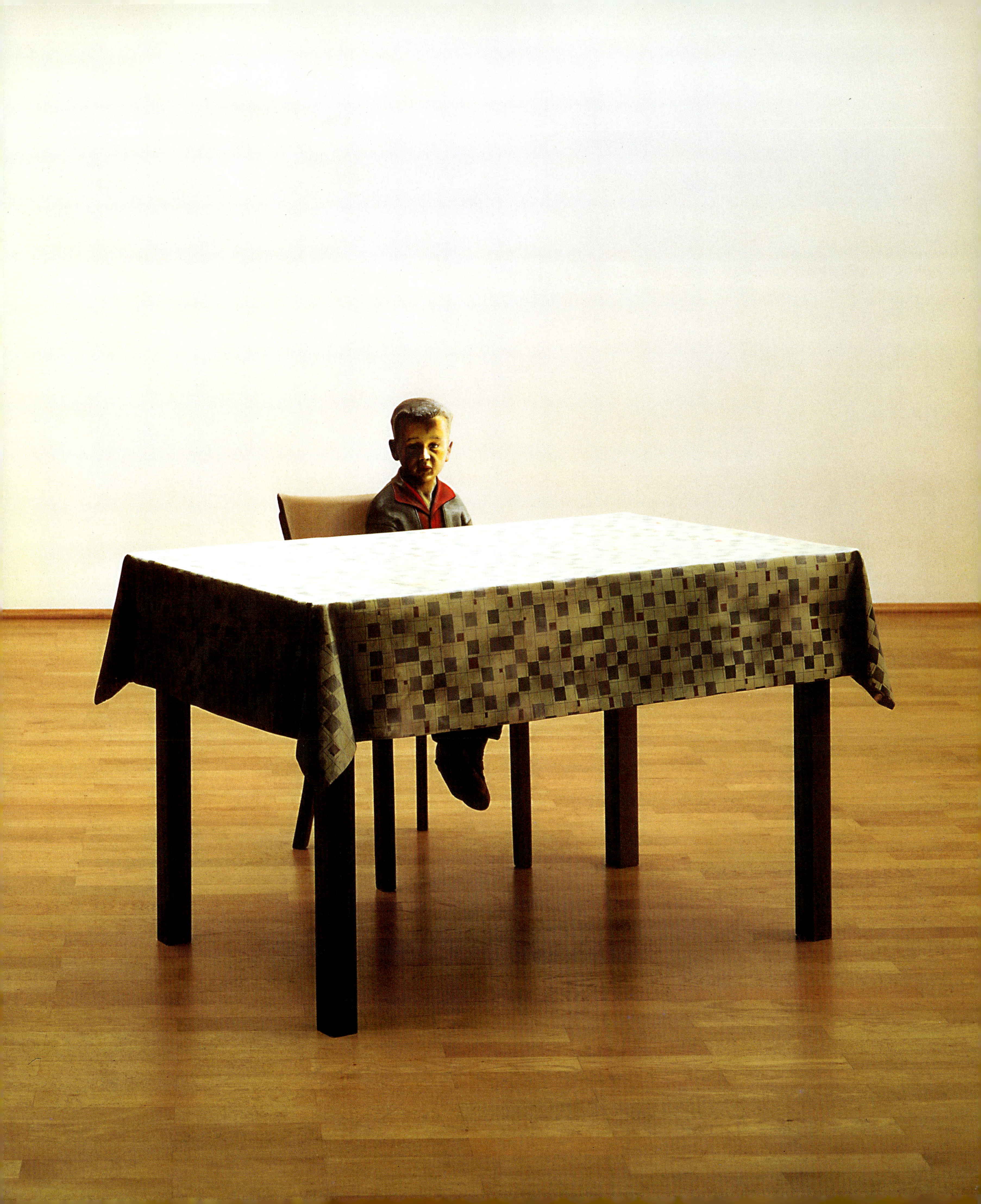

Fata Morgana (Mirage)
1996
epoxy, polyester, sand
image: 260 x 320 cm
sand castle: 240 x 180 cm

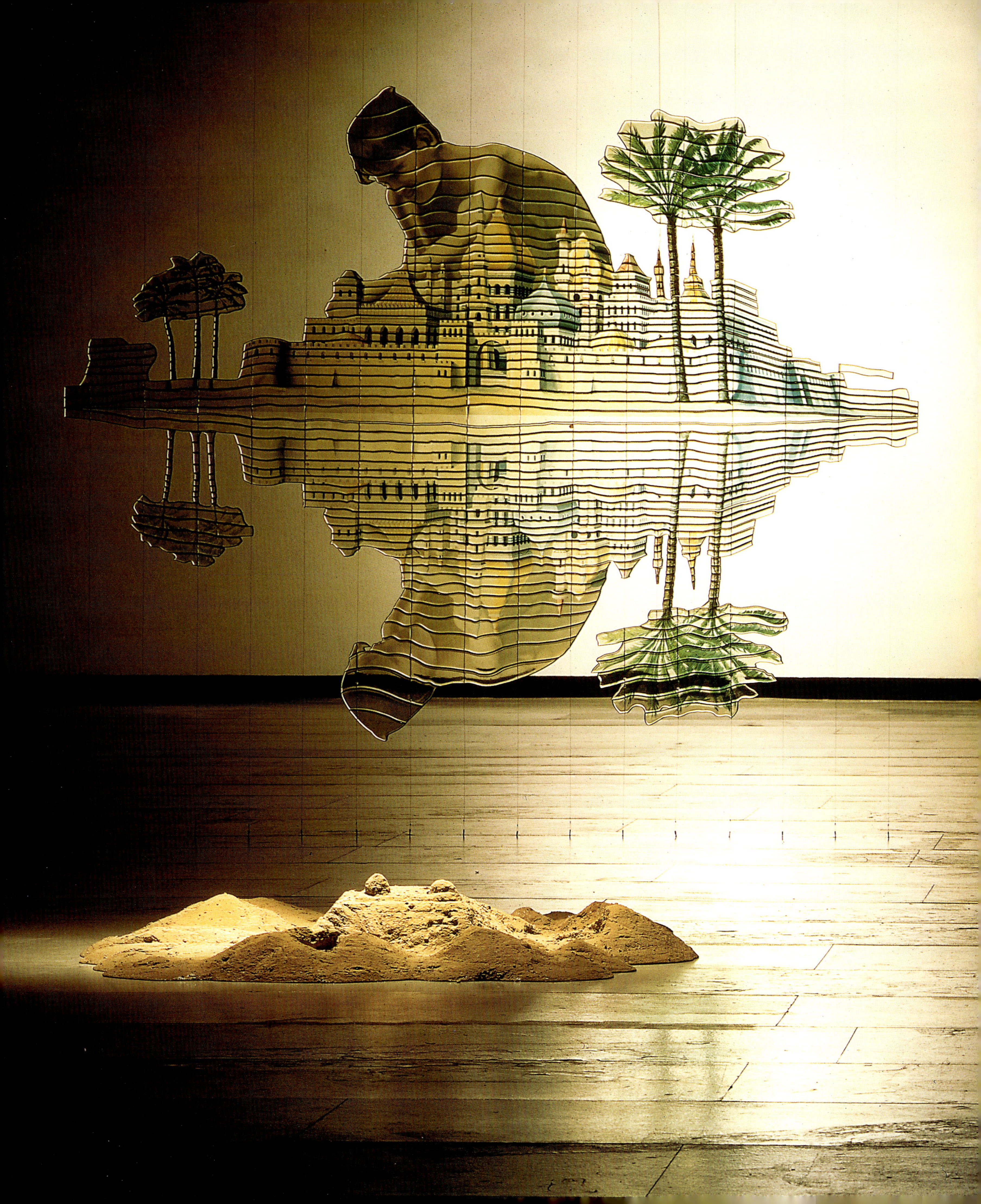

Thomas **RUFF**

Porträts
Stoya, P. Fries,
A. Siekeman, C. Pilar,
M. Schell, S. Kewer, M. Turk,
E. Zapp, A. Geise, O. Cleslik,
1986 – 1990
c-prints, plexiglass, wood
approx: 210 x 165 cm

anderes Porträts
(nos. 109A/11; 71A/92;
109/97; 122/113;
143/131; 104/109)
1994 – 1995
silkscreens on paper, glass, wood
200 x 150 cm

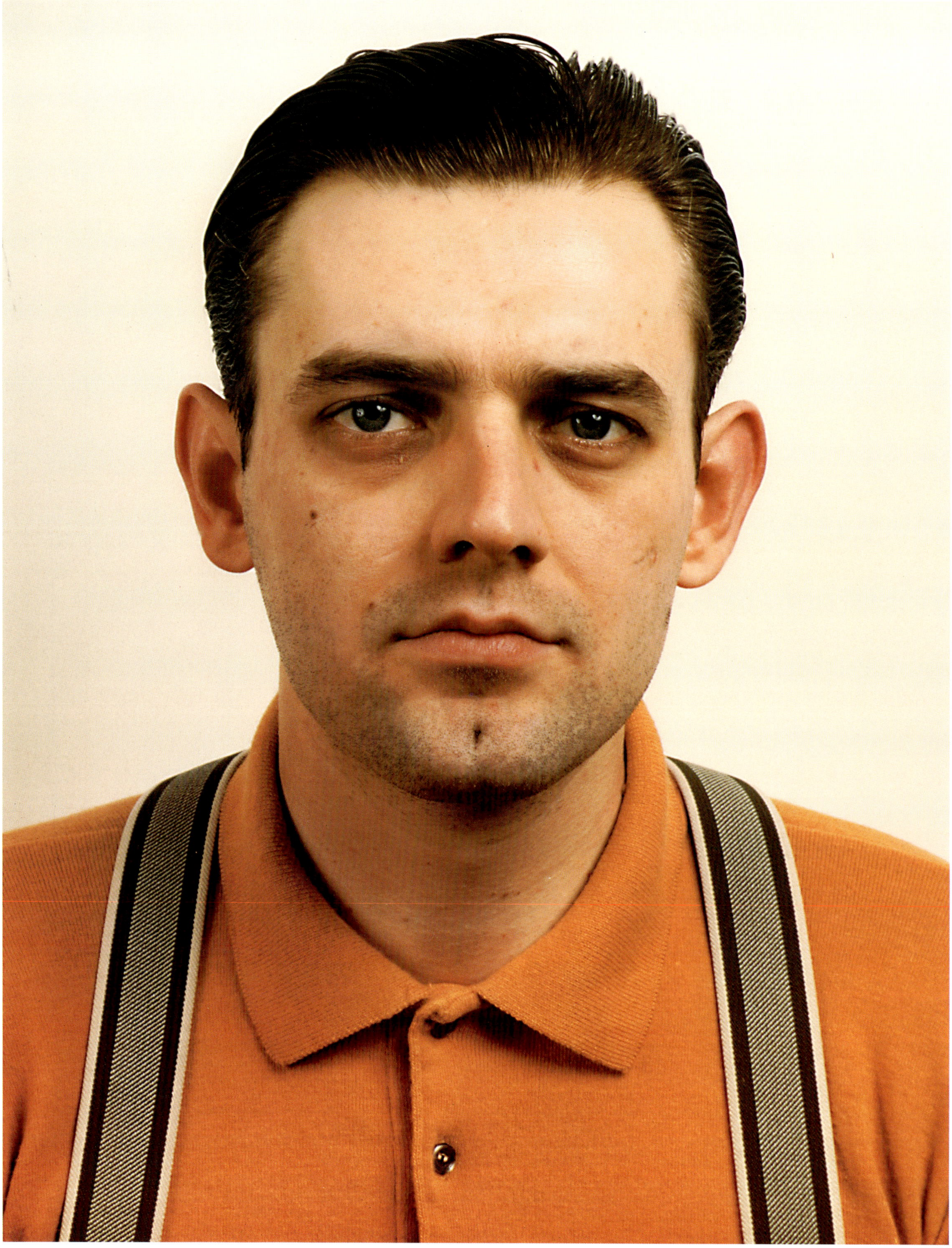

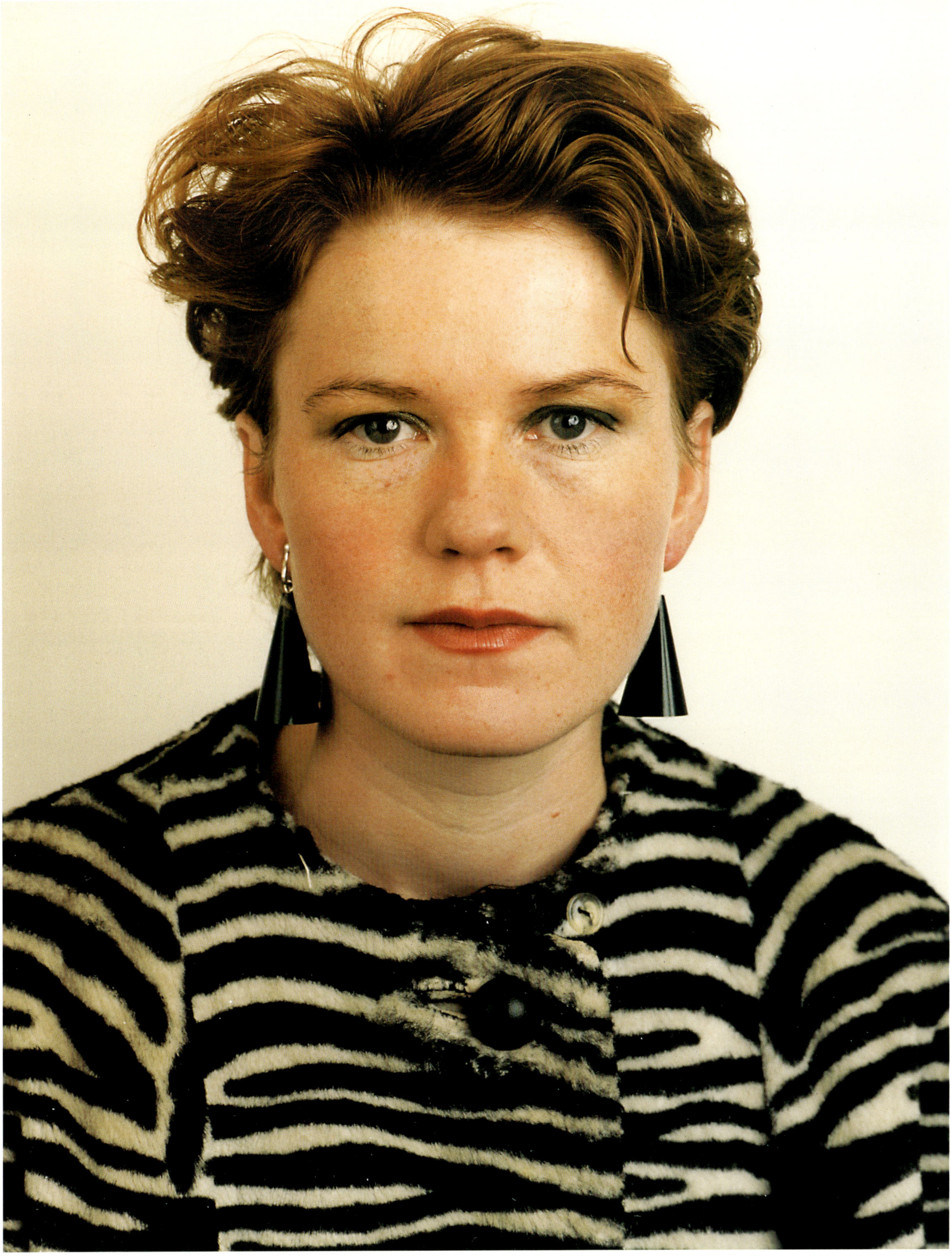

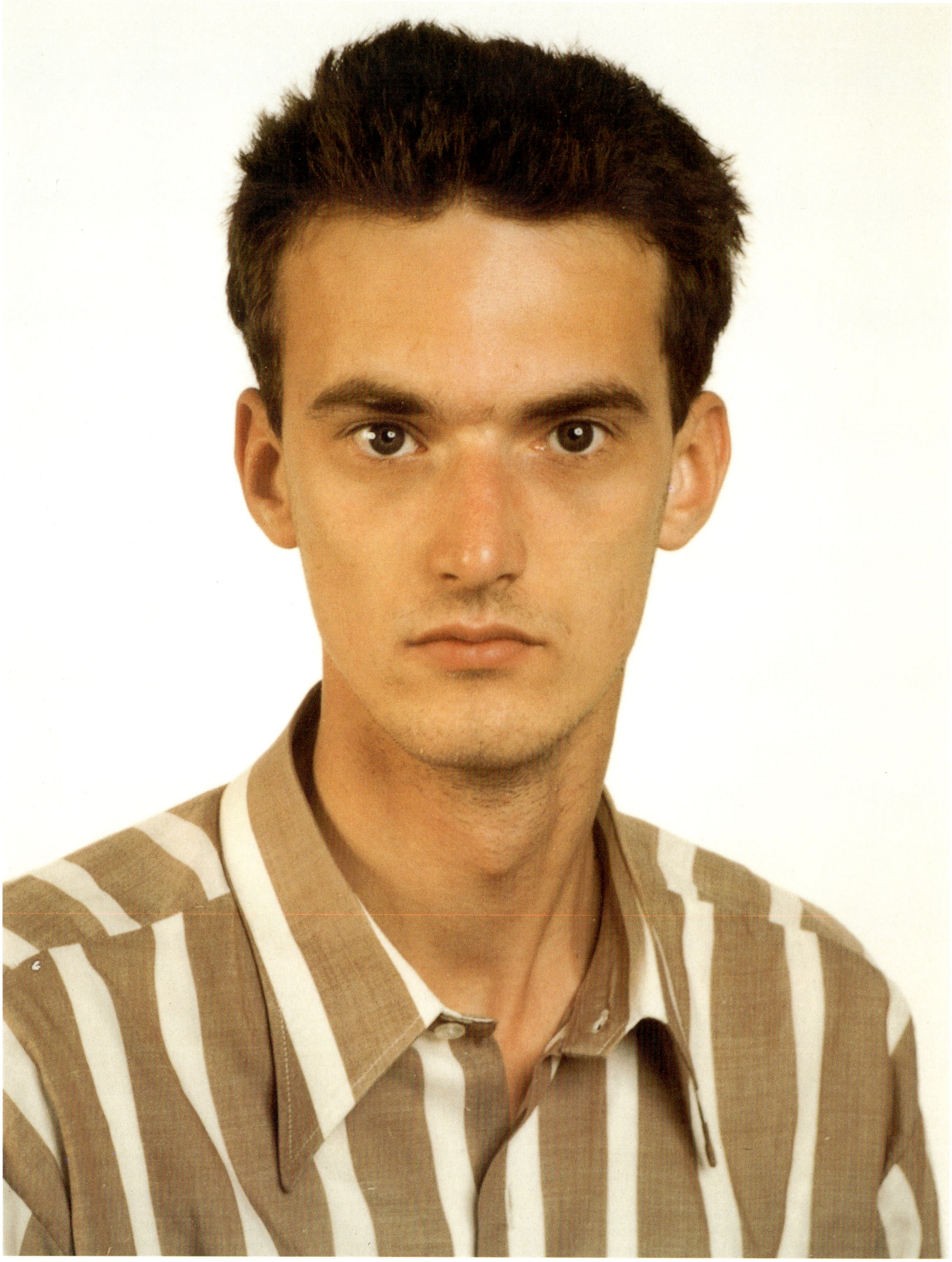

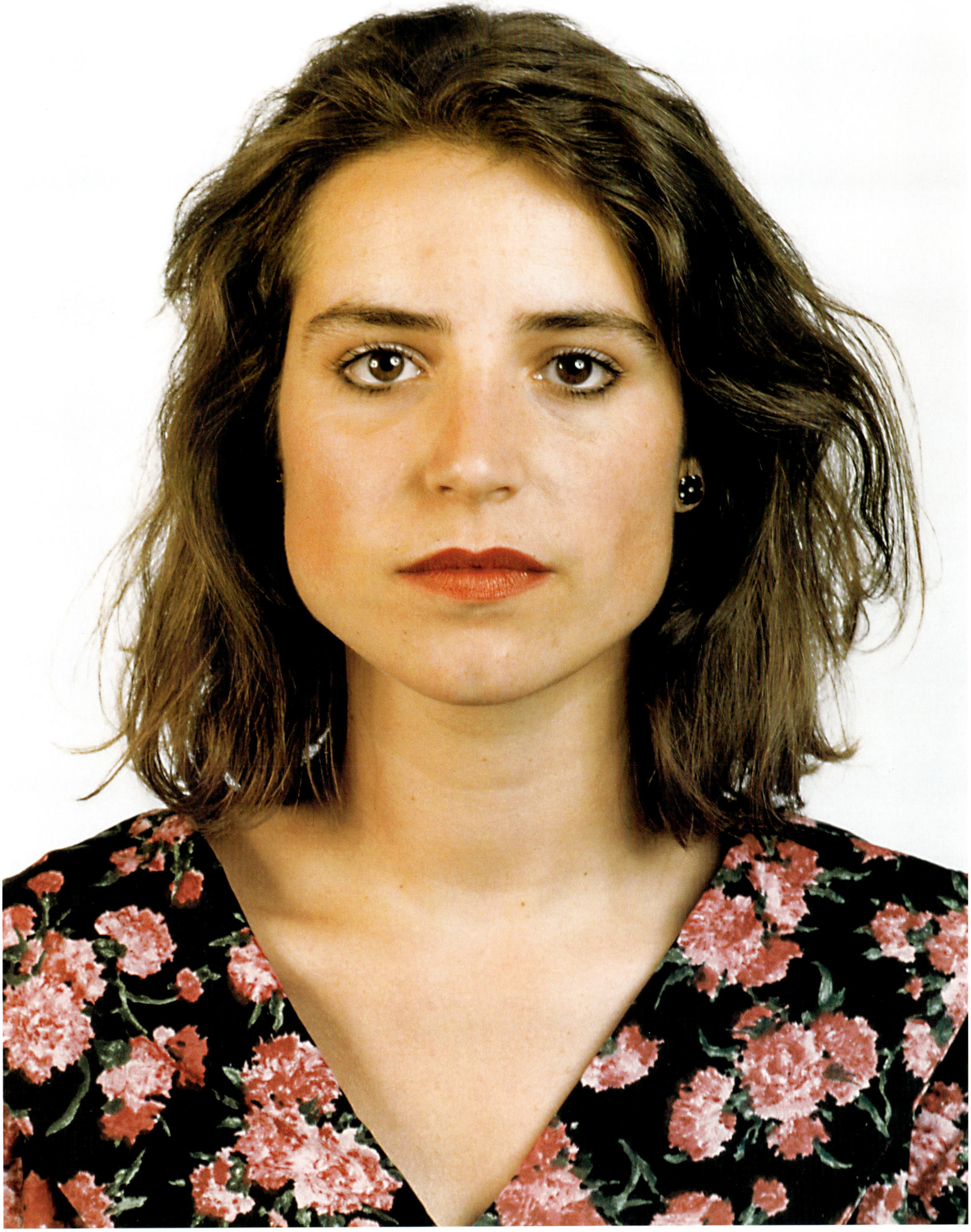

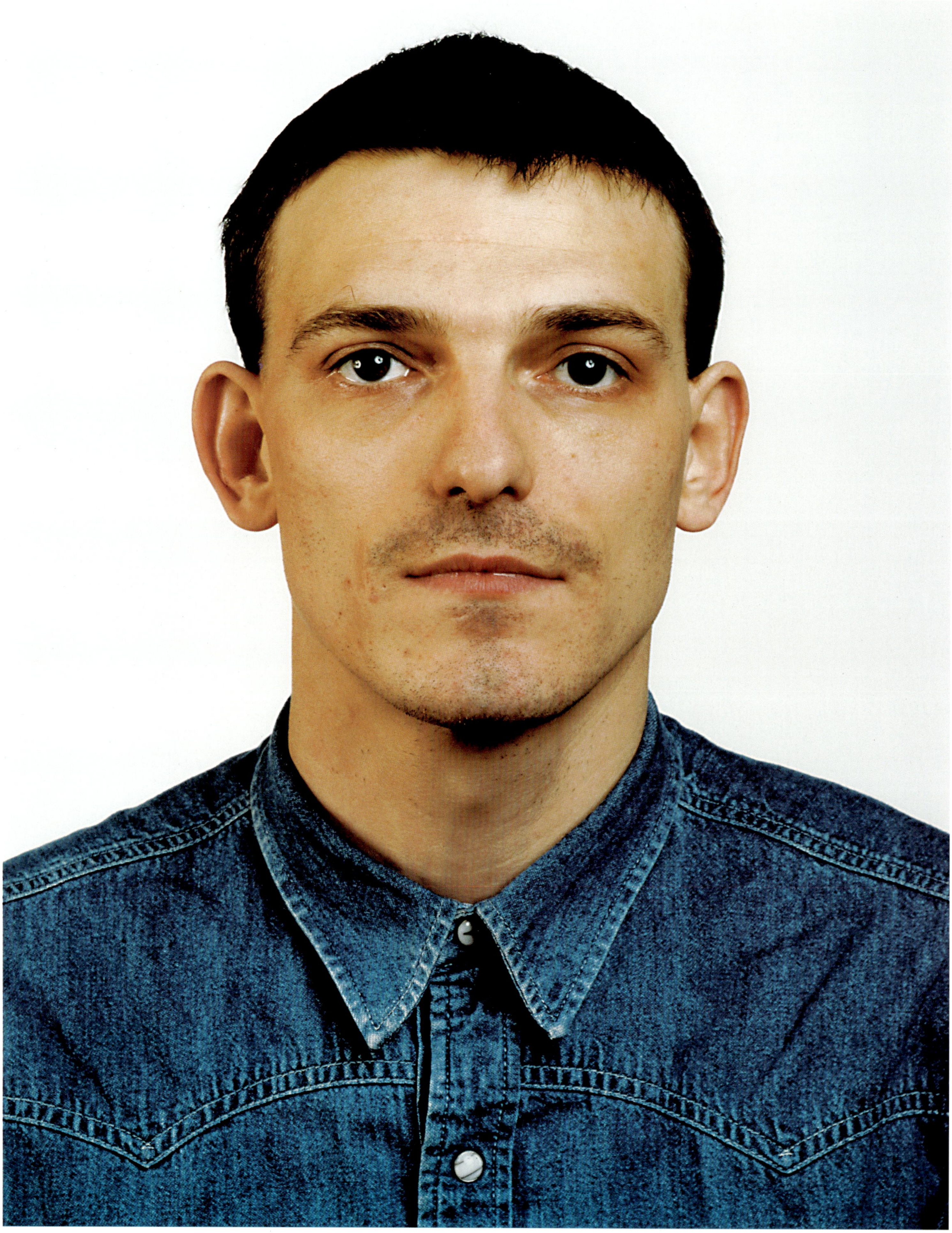

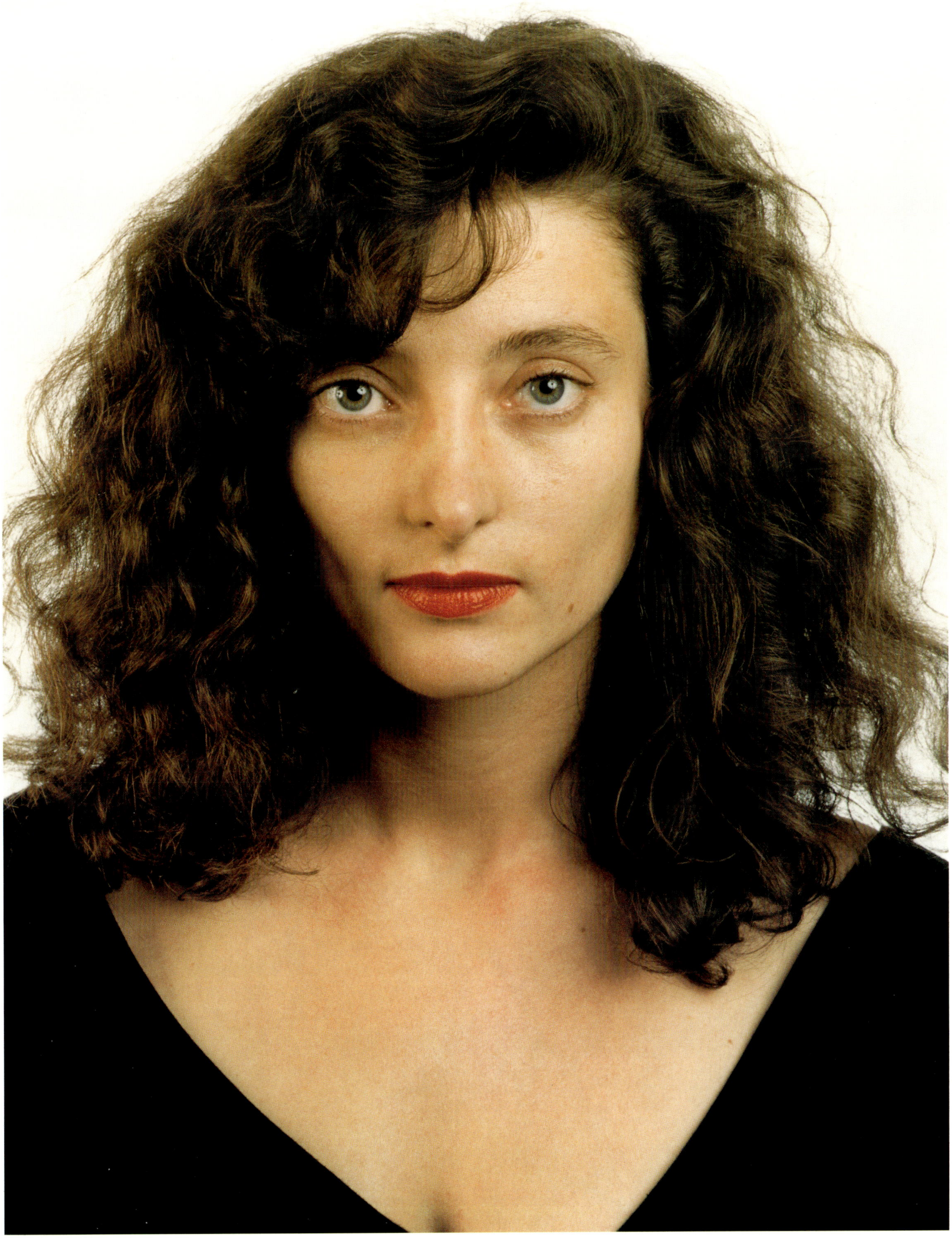

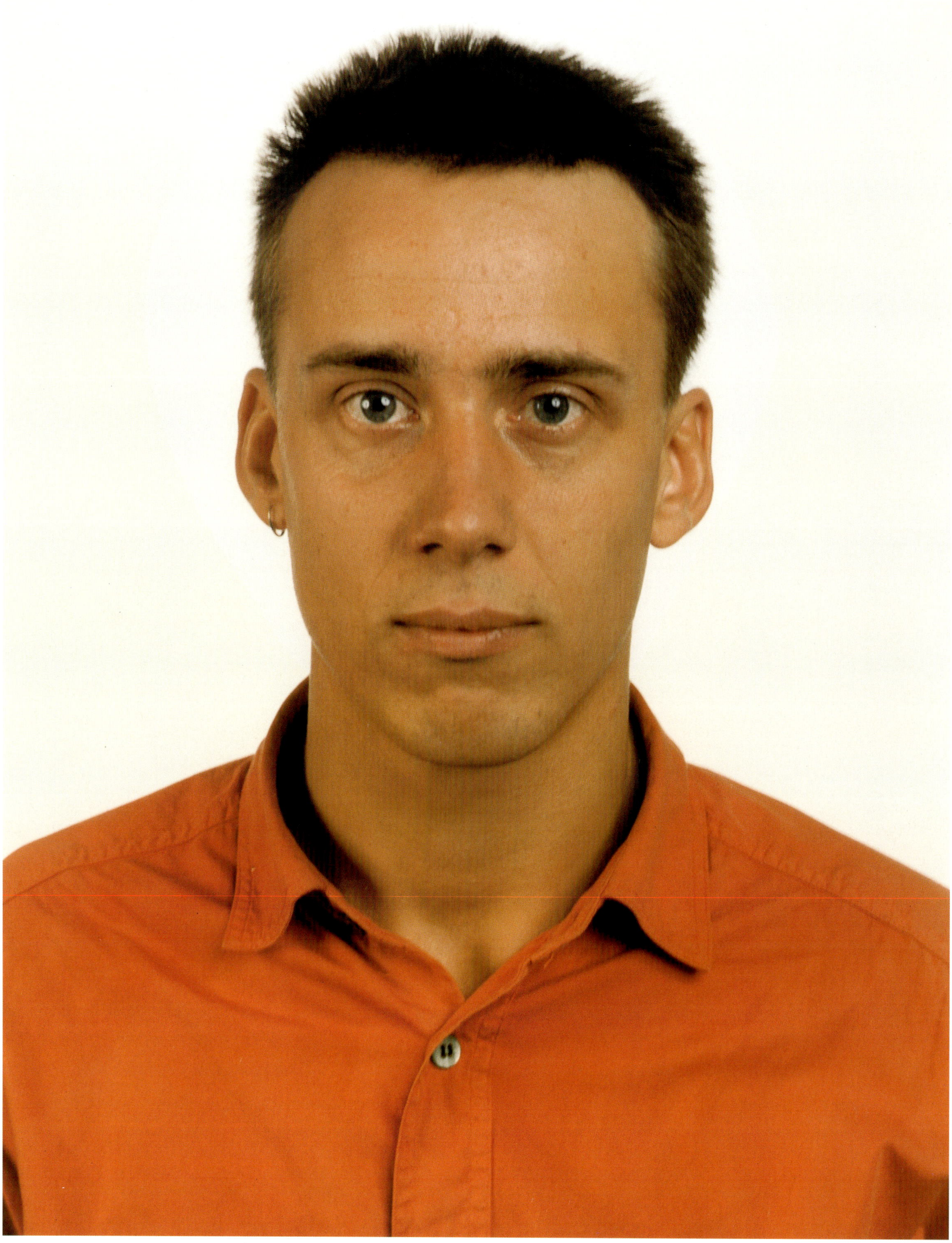

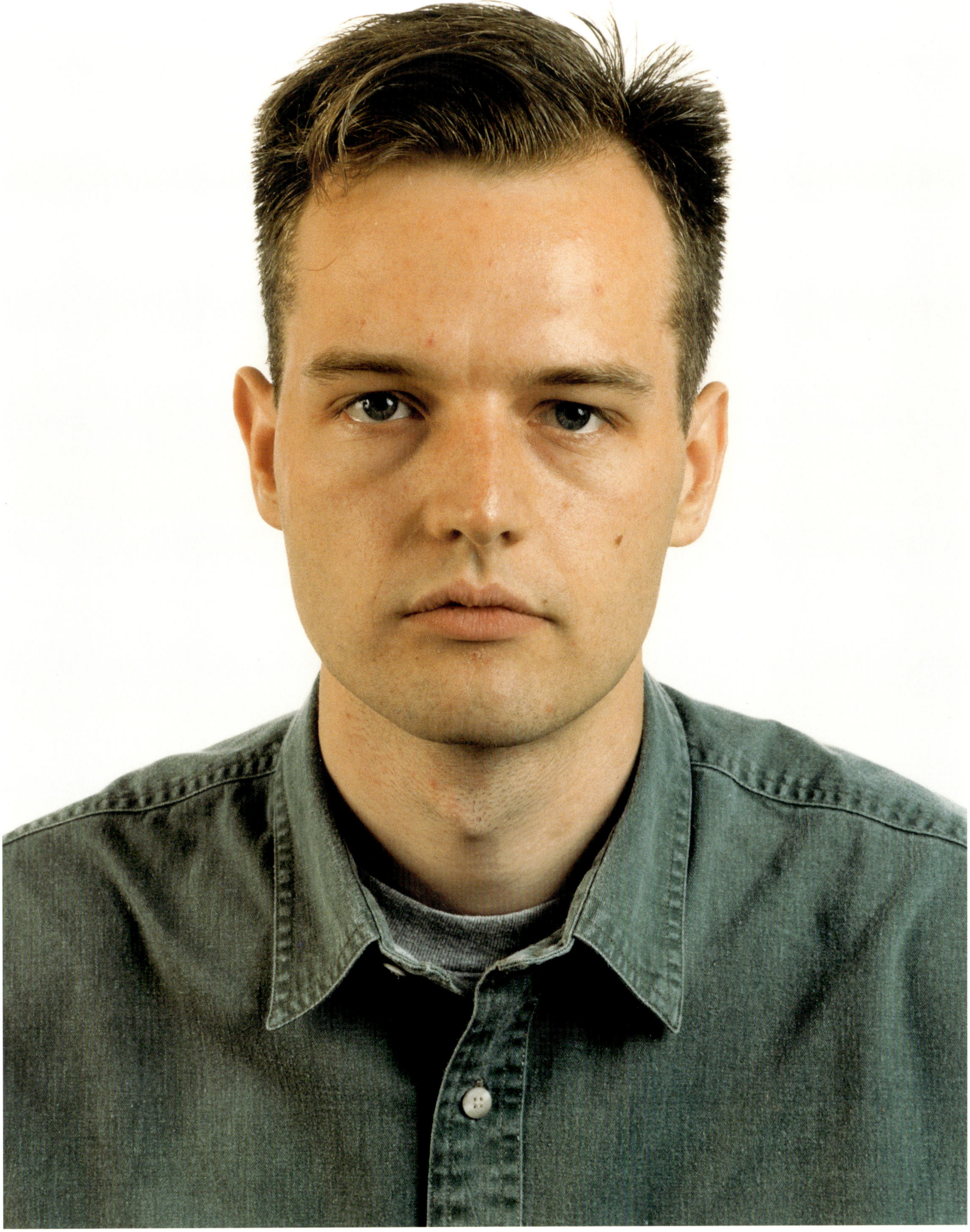

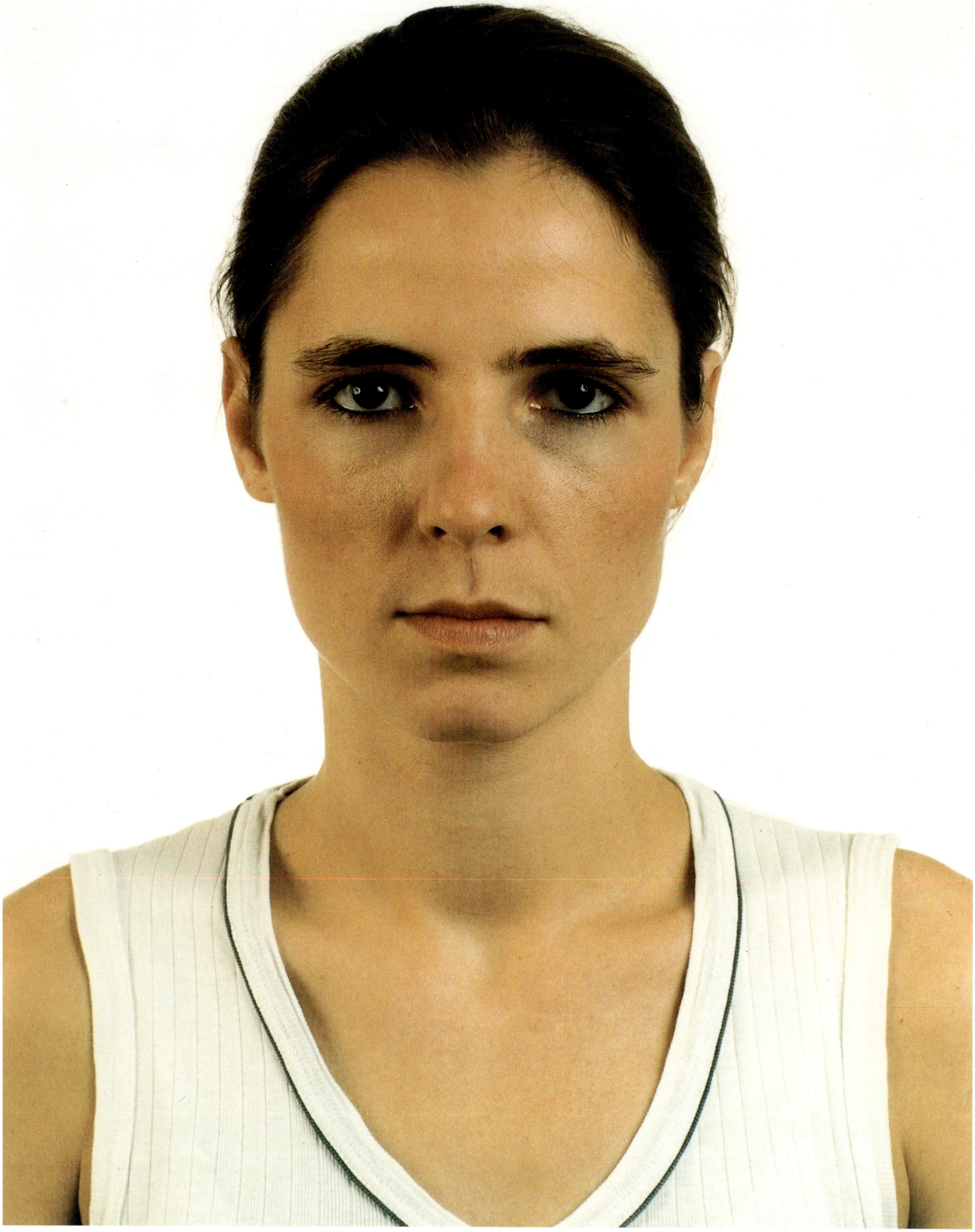

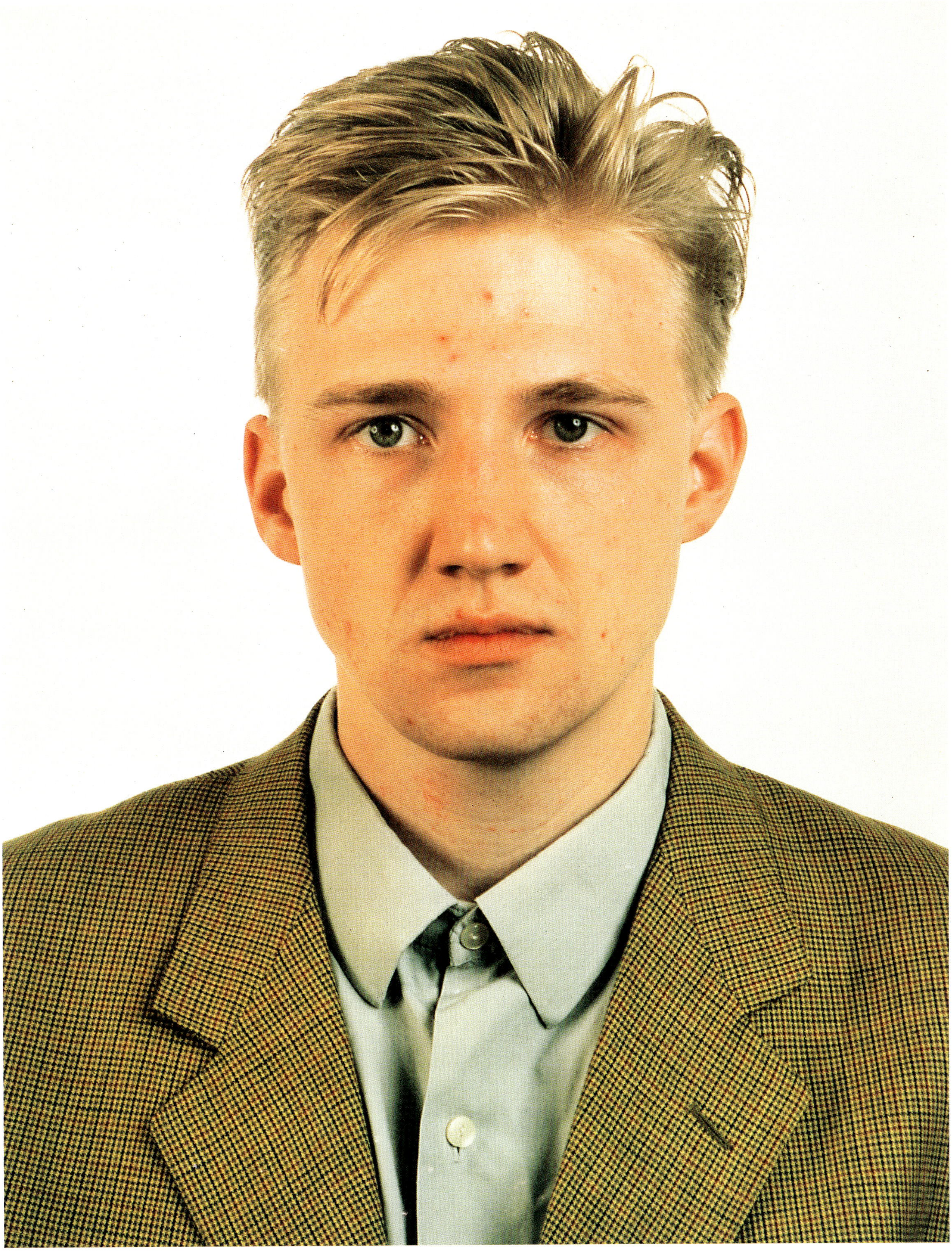

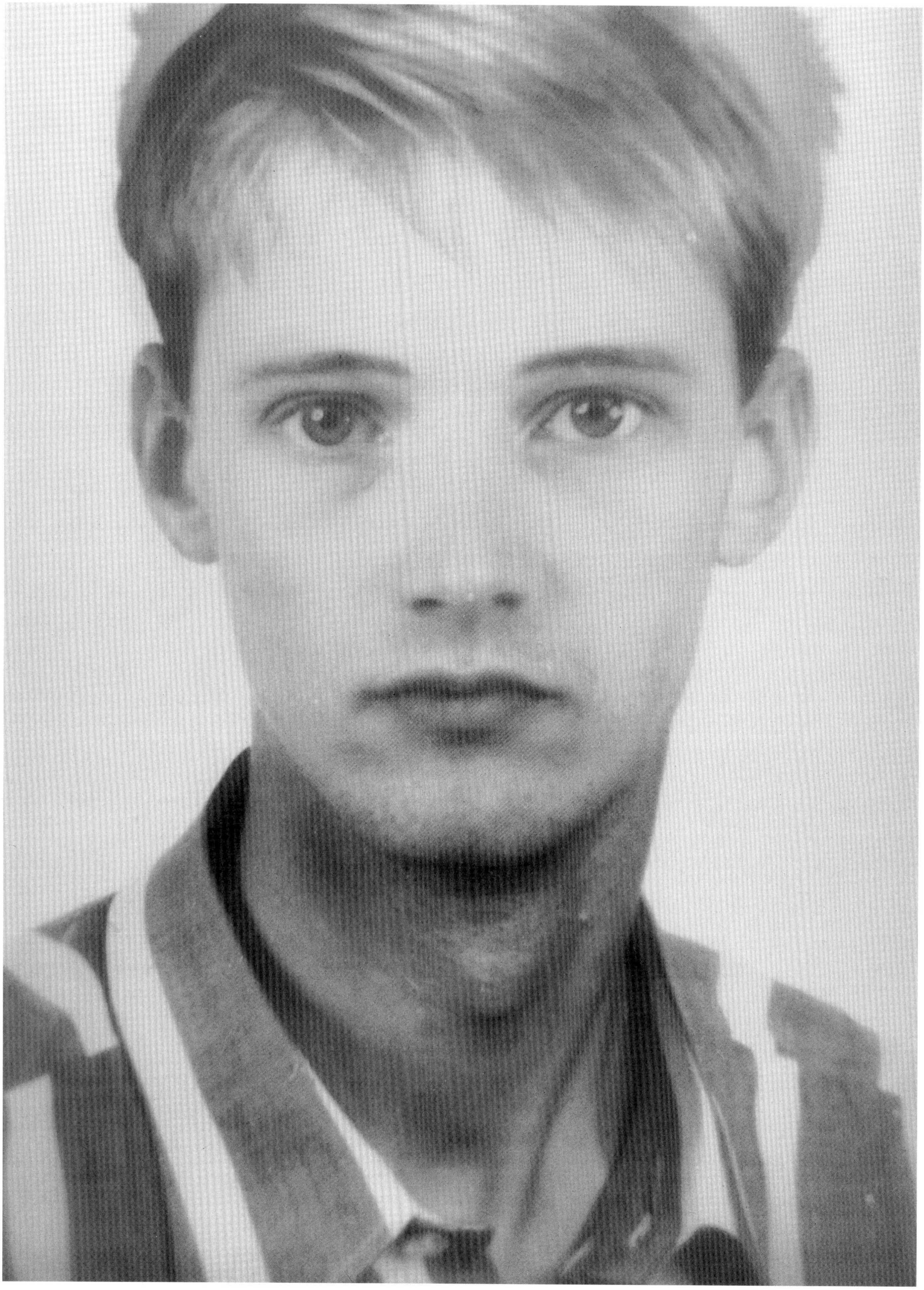

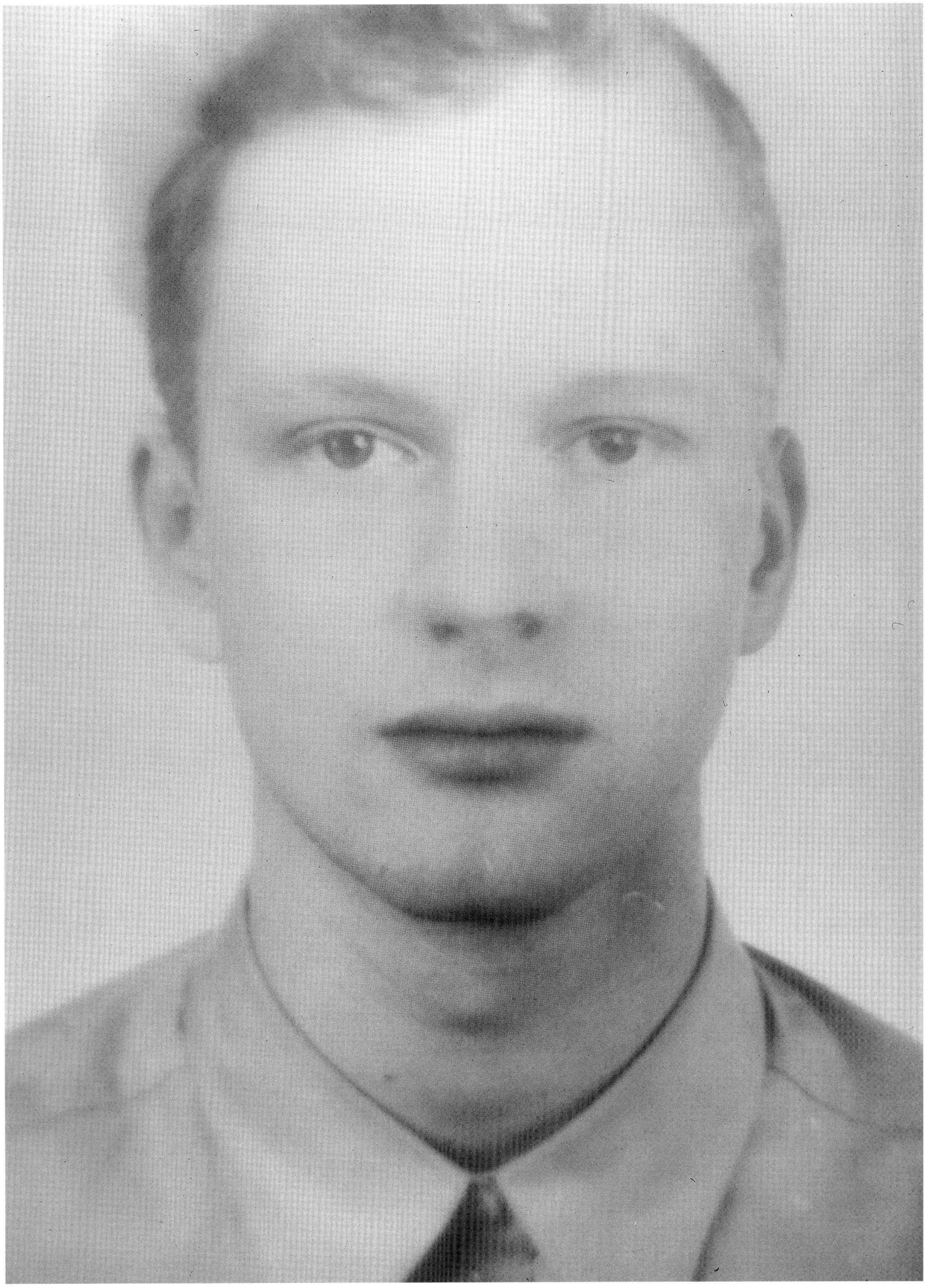

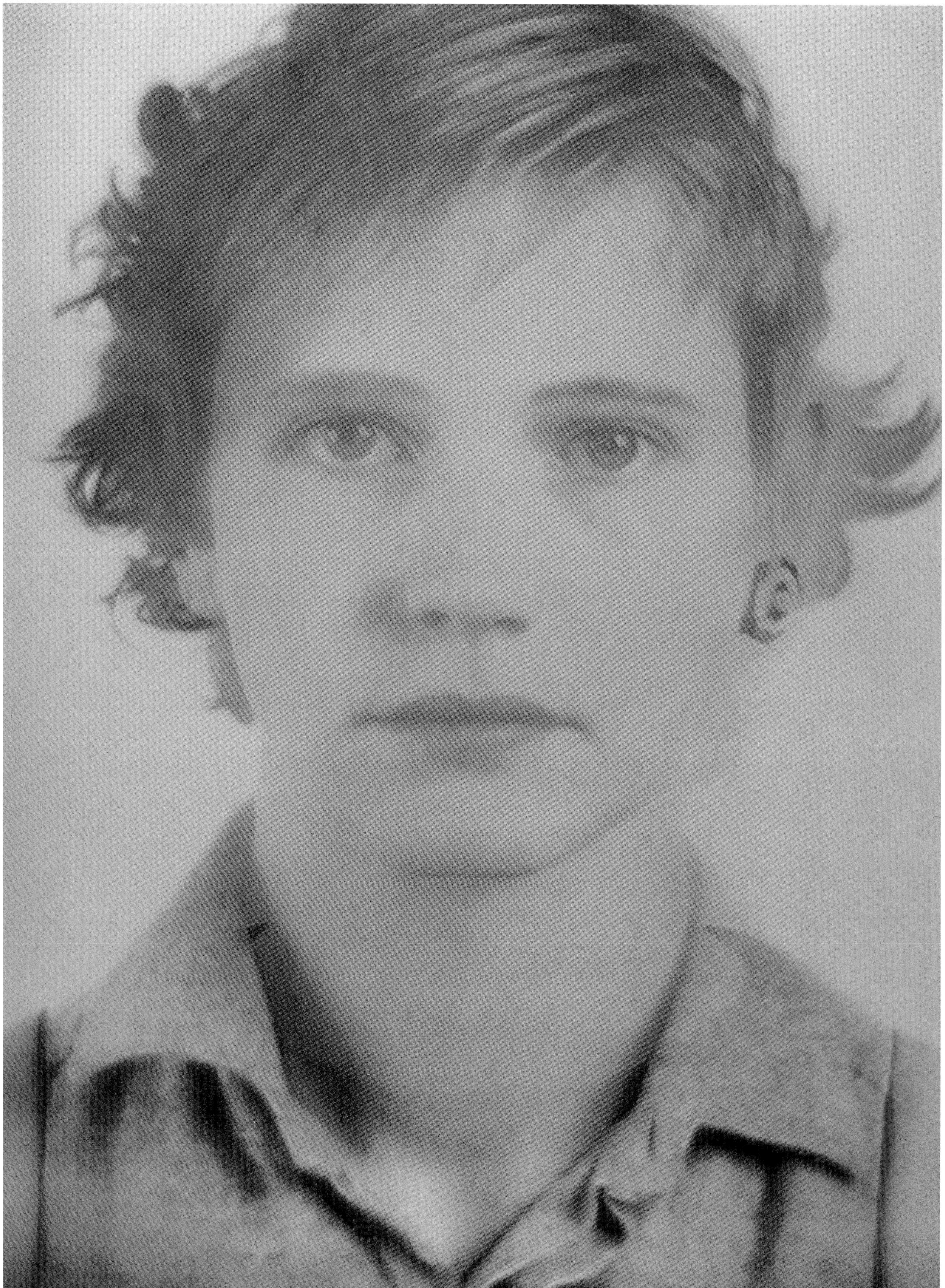

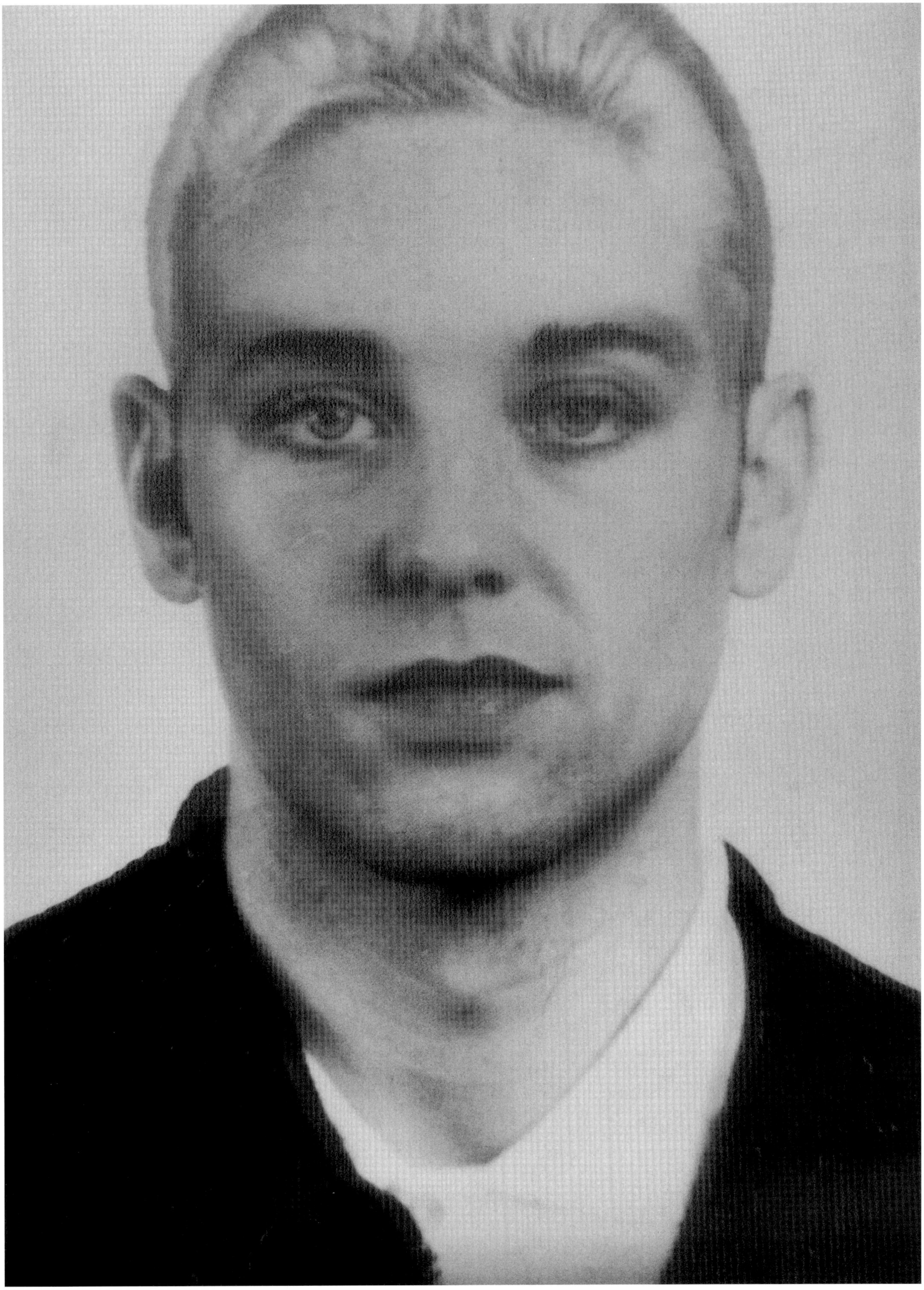

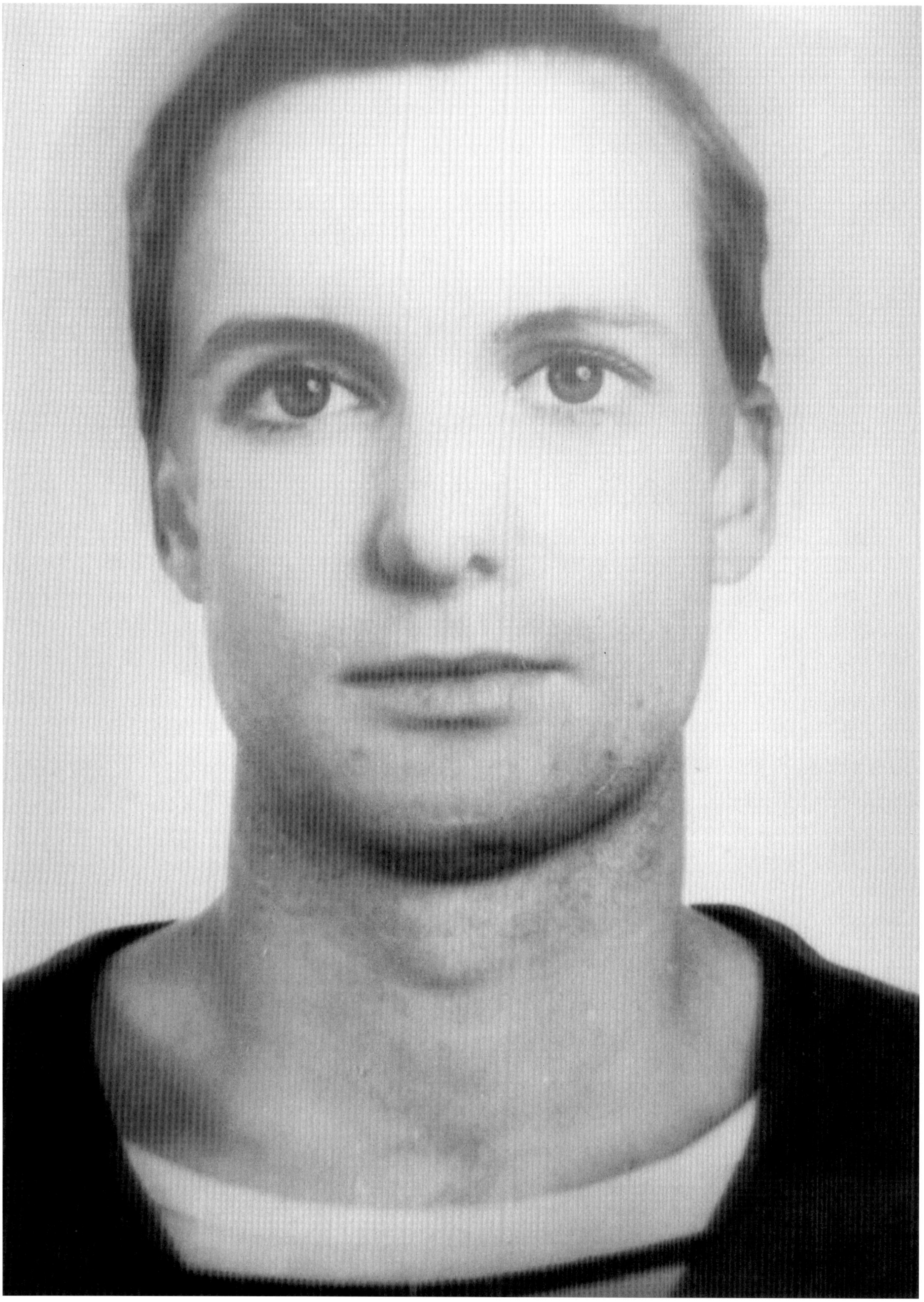

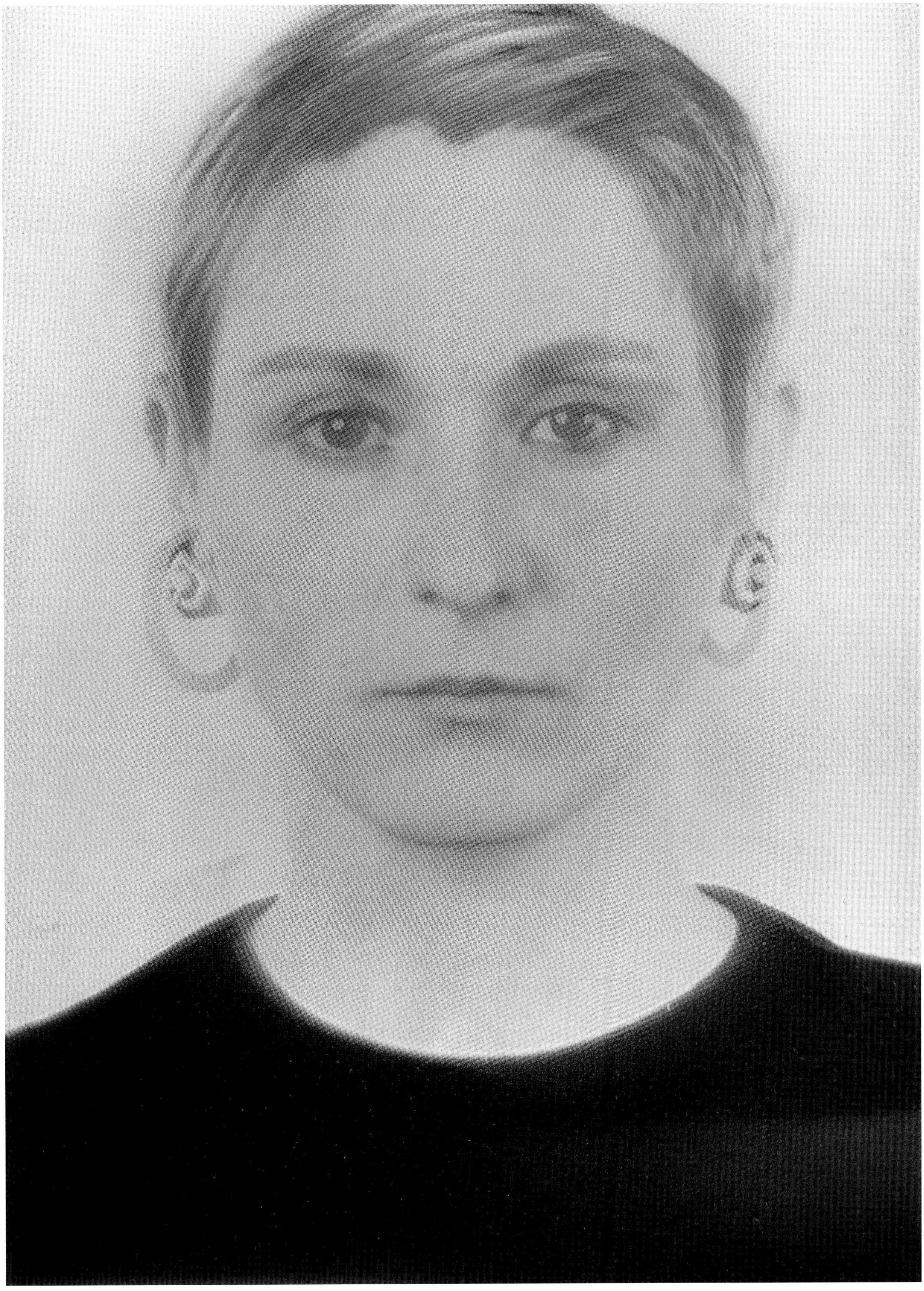

Thomas SCHÜTTE

Grosse Geister
1996
3 figures, cast aluminium
244 x 152 x 102 cm, 241 x 117 x 112 cm, 241 x 117 x 91 cm

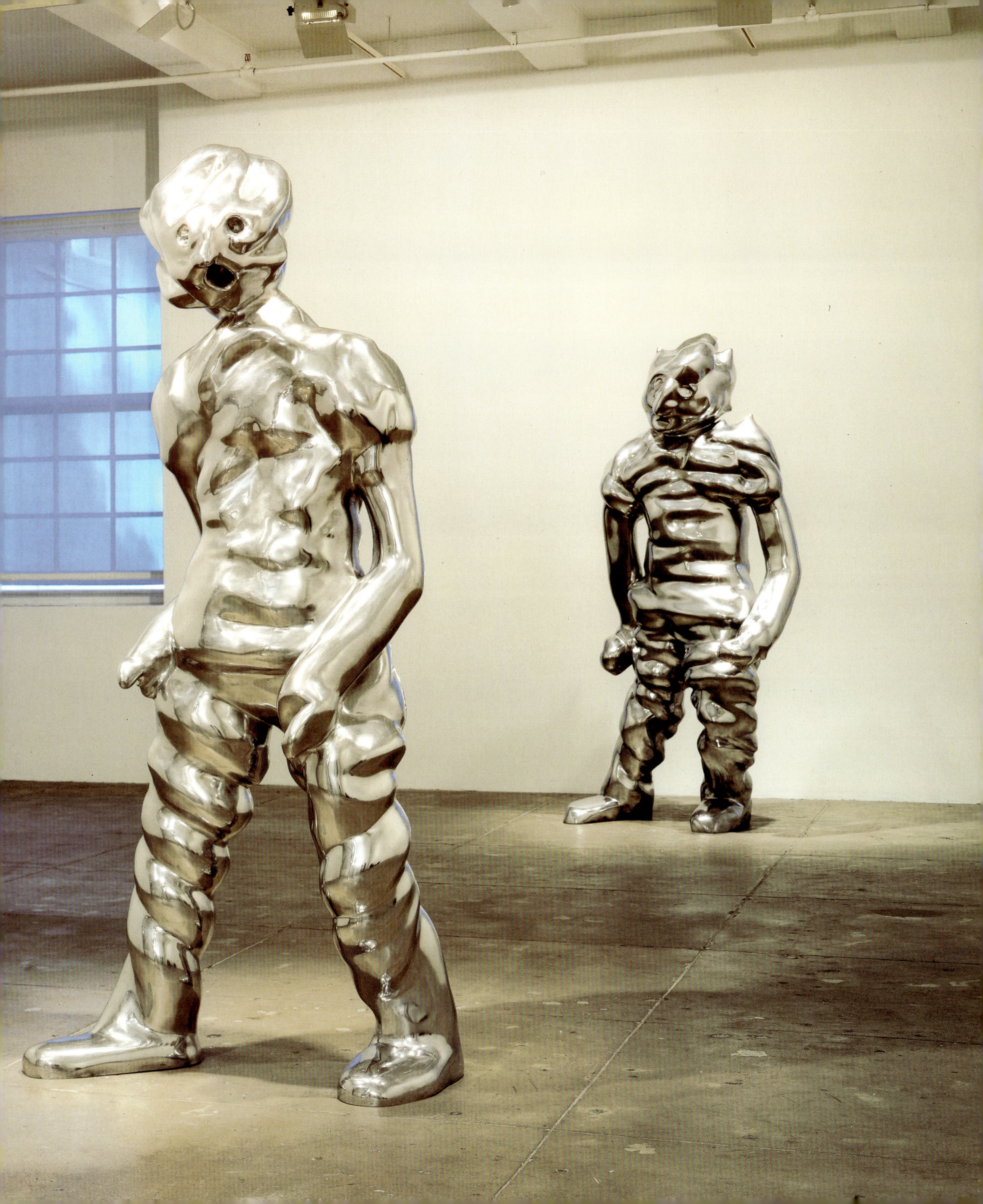

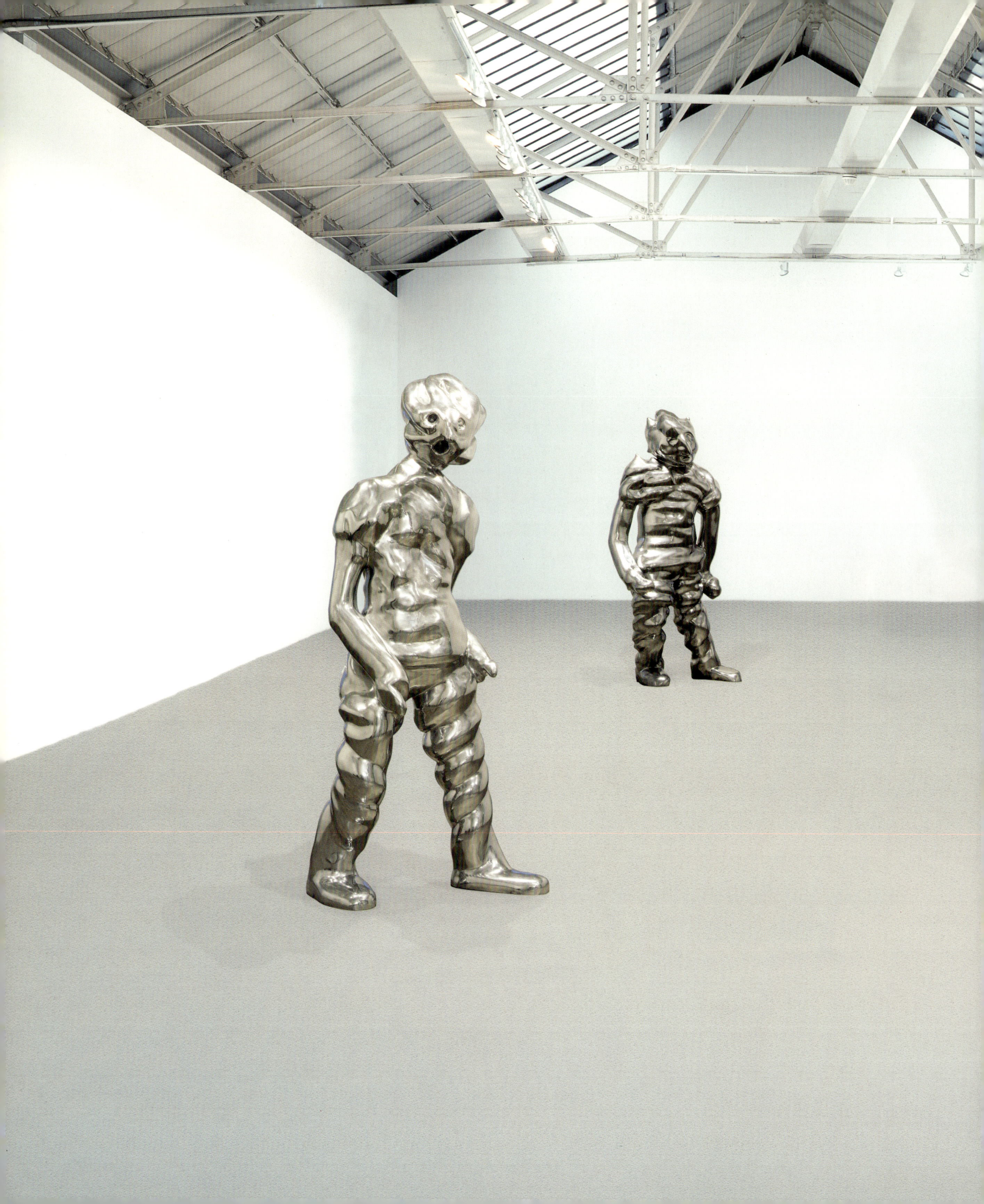

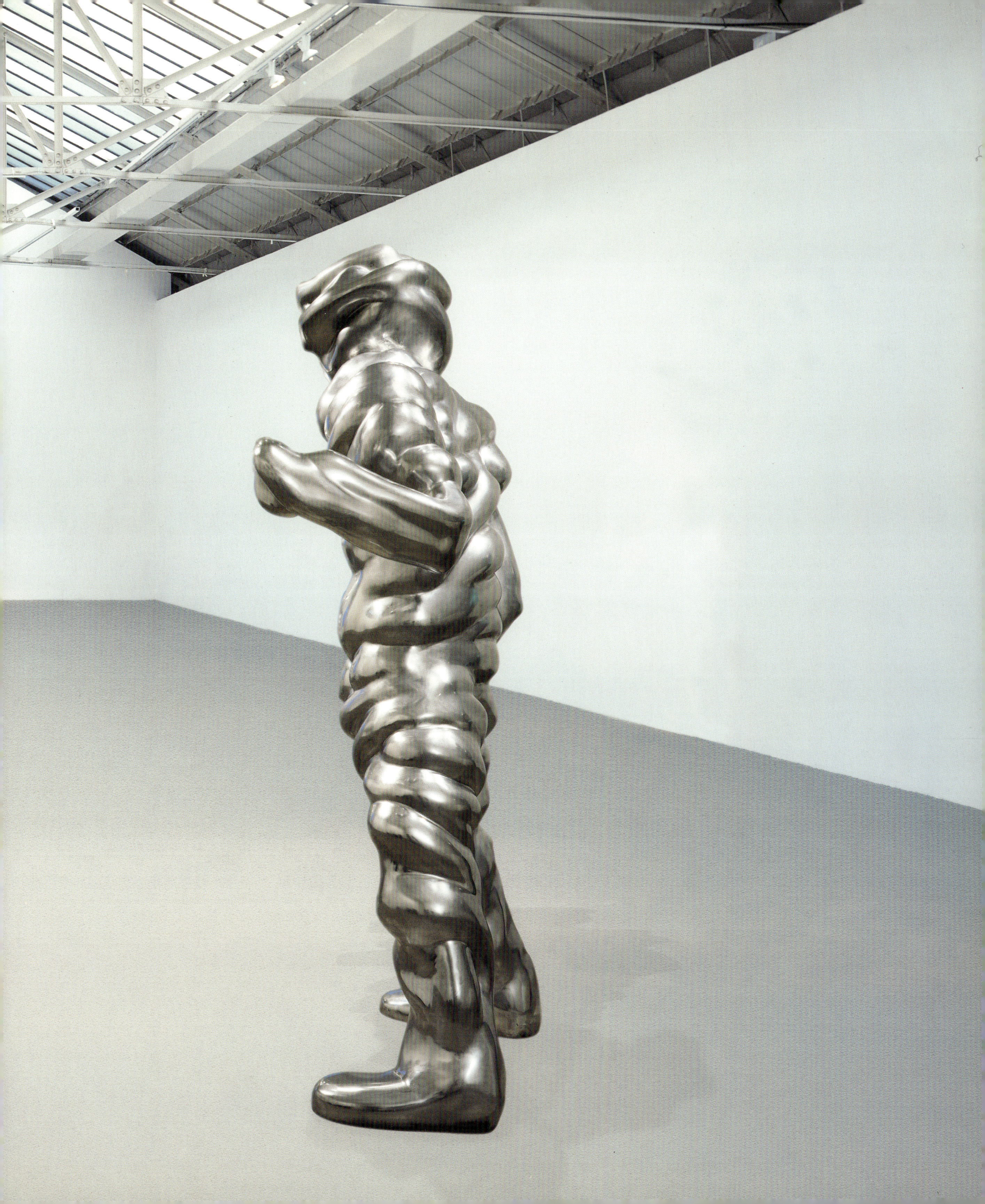

THOMAS GRÜNFELD

1958 Born in Opladen
1978–82 Studied at the Hochschule für Bildende Kunste, Stuttgart

Lives and works in Cologne

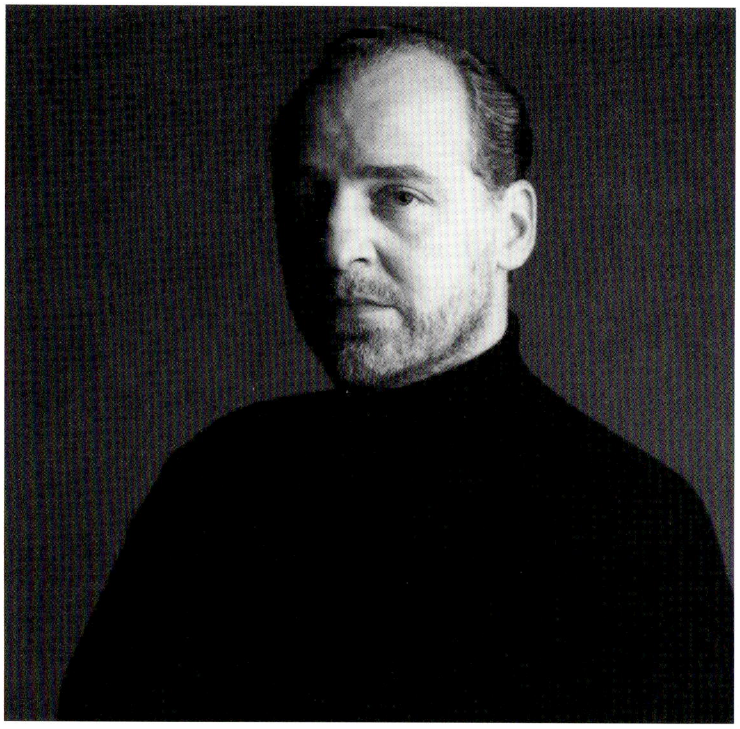

Solo Exhibitions

1980 Galerie Grunert Müller, Stuttgart
1982 Galerie Tanja Grunert, Stuttgart
1983 Galerie Schmitz & Becker, Duisburg
1984 Galerie Tanja Grunert, Cologne
1985 Ralph Wernicke Galerie, Stuttgart
1986 Galerie Tanja Grunert, Cologne
1987 XPO Galerie, Hamburg
Galerie Tanja Grunert, Cologne
1988 Massimo de Carlo, Milan
Jay Gorney Modern Art, New York (with Thomas Locher)
XPO Galerie, Hamburg (with Willi Kopf)
Interim Art, London
Karsten Schubert Ltd., London
Galerie Krinzinger, Vienna
1989 Galerie Tanja Grunert, Cologne
Ralph Wernicke Galerie, Stuttgart
1990 Karsten Schubert Ltd., London (with Thomas Locher)
XPO Galerie, Hamburg
Galerie Roger Pailhas, Marseille
Galerie Antoni Estrany, Barcelona
1991 Galerie Roger Pailhas, Paris
Massimo de Carlo, Milan
Galerie Ardi Poels, Maastricht
Galerie Tanja Grunert, Cologne
1992 Galerie Six Friedrich, Munich
Galerie Jousse Seguin, Paris
Casa de la Cultura, Santa Cruz, Teneriffa (with Andreas Schulze)
1993 Galerie Carstens, Berlin
Galerie Philomene Magers, Bonn
Galerie Ardi Poels, Maastricht
Galerie Jousse Seguin, Paris
1994 Galerie Ardi Poels, Maastricht
Galerie Jousse Seguin, Paris
1995 Galerie Antoni Estrany, Barcelona
Galerie im Taxispalais, Innsbruck
Galerie Michael Fuchs, Berlin
Galerie Ardi Poels, Maastricht
1996 Massimo de Carlo, Milano
Galerie Michael Janssen, Cologne
1997 Galerie Jousse Seguin, Paris
Karsten Schubert Ltd., London
Kolnischer Kunstverein, Cologne (with Rei Kawakubo)

Group Exhibitions

1989 *Aspects de la Jeune sculpture europeene*, Fondation Cartier, Paris
Prospect 89, Schirn Kunsthalle Franfurt
Kunst der letzeten 10 Jahre, Museum moderner Kunstm Vienna
D&S, Kunstverein Hamburg
Einleuchten; Will Vorstel und Simul in HH, Deichtorhallen Hamburg
1990 *Common Market*, Richard Kuhlenschmidt Gallery, Los Angeles
allo bell, allo sinistre, Artistes de Colonia, Centre d'Art Santa Monica, Barcelona
Aperto, Venice Biennale
1991 *10 Jahre Kunstfonds*, Kunstverein Bonn
Long Live the New Flesh, (Chadwick, Grunfeld, Serrano), Kettle's Yard, Cambridge
Anni Novanto, Galleria d'Arte Moderna, Bologne
Ars Usu, Haags Gemeentemuseum, The Hague
1992 *Avantgarde & Kampagne*, Kunsthalle Düsseldorf
Refusing to Surface, John Hansard Gallery, Southampton/Ikon Gallery, Birmingham/South London Art Gallery, London
Humpty Dumpty's Kaleidoscope, A New Generation of German Artists, Museum of Contemporary Art, Sydney
1968, Le Consortium, Dijon
1993 *The Last Garden*, Galleria d'Arte Moderna, Bologne
Kusnt um Kunst, (Grunfeld, Locher, Luckwald, Platino, Romer, Walz, Zimmerman), Kunsthalle Bieleefeld
Der 8. Tag, Oberosterreichisches Landesmuseum, Linz
Curlos & Miribillia, Chateau d'Oiron, Oiron
Alan Smithee, (Grunfeld, Jenney, Merz, Mucha, Patterson, Shine), Galeria Philomene Magers, Cologne
1994 *Das genre Tier*, Interimsgalerie der Kunstler, Munich
Kunstwerke e. v. Berlin
Grund: Works from the Collection, Museums Boymans – van Breunigen, Rotterdam
Nature Morte, Galerie Antoine da Galbert, Grenoble
Frankenstein: Exploration in Manipulations and Surrationality, MacDonald Stewart Art centre, Toronto
The Institute of Cultural Anxiety – Works from the Collection, Institute of Contemporary Art, London
1995 *Disneyland after Dark*, Kuntmeseum Uppsala
1996 *Private View*, Bowes Museum, Barnard Castle, Co. Durham
Happy end, Kunsthalle Düsseldorf
Hybrids, Stichting de Appel, Amsterdam
Siafo, Exhibition Centre, Seoul
1997 *Wandstucks IV*, Galerie Bob van Orsouw, Zürich
Plastik, Wurtembergischer Kunstverein, Stuttgart
Home Sweet Home, Deichtorhallen, Hamburg

ANDREAS GURSKY

1955 Born Leipzig
1977–80 Studied at Gesamthochschule, Essen
1980–87 Studied at Staatliche Kunstakademie, Düsseldorf

Lives and works in Düsseldorf

Solo Exhibitions

1987 Flughafen Düsseldorf
1988 Galerie Johnen & Schottle, Cologne
1989 Centre Genevois de Gravure Contemporaine, Geneva
P.S.1. the Clocktower Gallery, Long Island, New York (with Thomas Struth)
303 Gallery, New York
Museum Haus Lange, Krefeld
1991 Galerie Rudiger Schottle, Munich
Galerie Johnen & Schottle, Cologne
303 Gallery, New York
Galerie Rudiger Schottle, Paris
Kunstlerhaus Stuttgart
1992 Kunsthalle Zürich
Victoria Miró Gallery, London
Galleria Lia Rumma, Naples
1993 Monika Spruth Galerie, Cologne
1994 Deictorhallen, Hamburg
De Appel Foundation, Amsterdam
Le Case d'Arte, Mailand
1995 303 Gallery, New York
Lumen Travo, Amsterdam
Rooseum-Center for Contemporary Art, Malmo
Tate Gallery, Liverpool
Galeried Mai 36, Zürich
Fortikus, Frankfurt
1996 Galerie Jean Bernier, Athens
Galerie Ghislaine Hussenor, Paris
Victoria Miró Gallery, London
Monika Spruth Galerie, Cologne

Selected Group Exhibitions

1986 Galerie Rudiger Schottle, Munich
1988 Galerie Johnen
1989 Lenbachhaus, Munich
In Between and Beyond – From Germany, Power Plant Museum, Toronto
1990 *Aperto*, Venice Biennale
1991 *10 Jahre Kunstfonds*, Kunstverein Bonn
Aus der Distanz, Kunstsammlung Norfrhein-Westfalen, Düsseldorf
Squardo di Medusa, Castello di Rivoli
Bremer Art Prize, Kunsthalle Bremen
1992 *Double Take: Collective Memory & Current Art*, Hayward Gallery, London
Qui, Quoi, Ou? Un regard sur l'arten Allemagne en 1992, Musée d'Art Moderne de la Ville de Paris
1993 *Die photographie in der deutschen Gegenwartskunst*, Museum Ludwig, Cologne
Distanz und Nahe, Nationalgalerie, Berlin
1994 *The Epic and the Everyday*, Hayward Gallery, London
1995 Fotografiska Museet, Stockholm (with Willie Doherty)
1996 *Prospect '96*, Schirn Kunsthalle, Frankfurt
1997 *Belladonna*, ICA, London

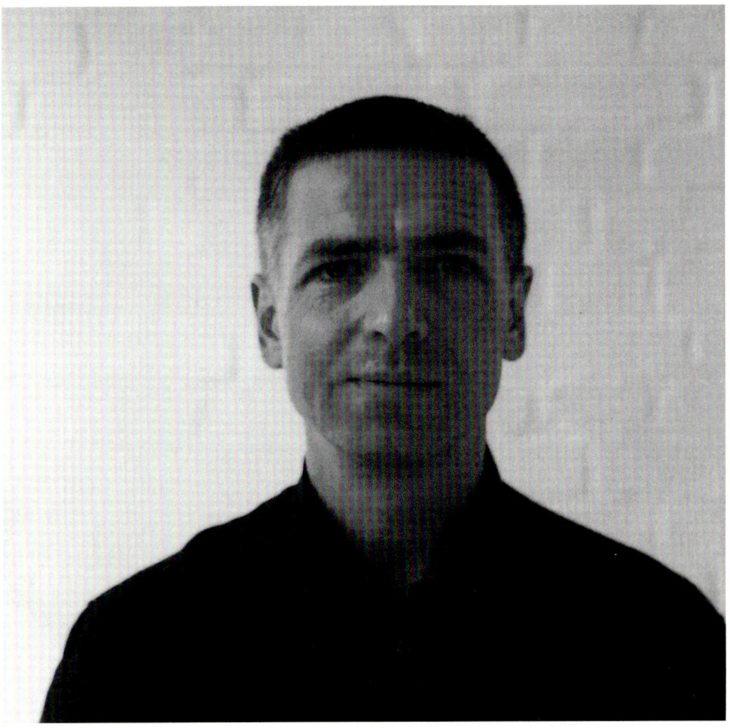

STEFAN HABLÜTZEL

1964	Born Bern, Switzerland
1985–91	Studied at the Kunstakademie Düsseldorf
	Lives and works in Düsseldorf

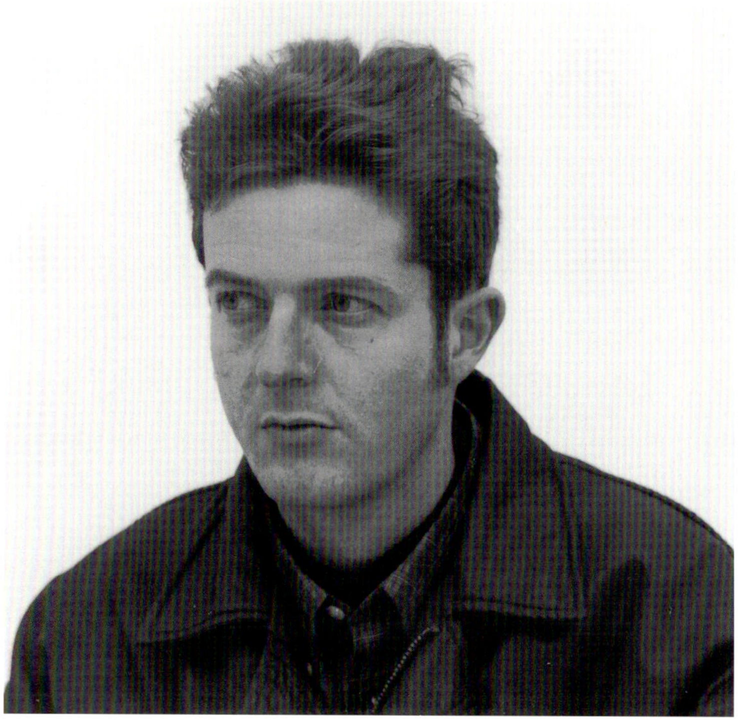

Exhibitions

1990	Eidgenossisches Kunststpendium
1991	Eidgenossisches Kunststpendium
1992	Eidgenossisches Kunststpendium
	Stefan Hablützel, Callum Innes, Corinne Wasmuht, Galerie Johnen & Schottle, Cologne
1994	Elke Denda, Stefan Hablützel, Martin Honnert, Daniel Oates, Galerie Johnen & Schottle, Cologne
	Auf eigene Gefahr, Bonn
1996	*Fondo, Figura Y Lluvia*, Gallery Antoni Estrany, Barcelona (curated by Jose Lebrero Staals)
1997	*1962/1929*, Galerie Johnen & Schottle, Cologne

MARTIN HONERT

1953 Born in Bottrop
1981–88 Studied in Staatliche Kunstakademie Düsseldorf
1985 Masterclass with Fritz Schwegler

Lives and works in Düsseldorf

Solo Exhibitions

1988 Galerie Johnen & Schottle, Cologne
Galerie Schottle, Munich (with Elke Denda)
1990 Galerie Johnen & Schottle, Cologne
1991 Galerie Schottle, Munich
Bonner Kunstverein, Peter-Mertes-Stipendium
1996 *Zuspiel. Martin Honert und Stefan Hoderlein*, Siemens Kulturprogramm, Wurttembergischer Kunstverein. Stuttgart and Arnolfini Gallery, Bristol, GB (*Das fliegende Kiassenzimmer*)

Selected Group Exhibitions

1989 Stichting de Appel, Amsterdam (with Katharina Fritsch and Thomas Ruff)
1990 *Carnet de Voyage*, Fondation Cartier, Jouy-en-Josas, France
1991 *Art conceptuel des annees 79 à aujourd'hui*, Galerie Rudiger Schottle, Paris, France
Anni '90, Galleria Comunale d'Arte Moderna, Bologne/Cattolica/Rimini, Italy
1992 *Double Identity*, Galerie Johnen & Schottle, Cologne
Biennale of Sydney, Sydney, Australia
Post Hurnan, Musée d'Art Contemporain, Pully/Lausanne, Switzerland; Castello di Rivara, Rivara-Turin, Italy; Deste Foundation, Athens, Greece; Deichtorhallen, Hamburg
Renta Preis, Nürnberg
Elisabeth-Schneider-Stiftung, Freiburg
Qui, quoi, ou?, Un regard sur l'art en Allemagne en 1992, Musée d'Art Moderne de la Ville de Paris, Paris, France
Museum für Moderne Kunst, Frankfurt/Main
1993 Galerie Massimo de Carlo, Mailand, Italy
APERTO, Venice Biennale, Italy
Menschenwelt (Interieur), Portikus Frankfurt/Main; Castello di Rivara, Rivara-Turin, Italy; Norwich Gallery, Norfolk Institute of Art and Design, Norfolk; Wurttembergischer Kunstverein Stuttgart; Westfalischer Kunstverein Munster
Kunstpreis der Bottcherstrasse in Bremen, Bremen
1994 Kunsthaus Murzzuschlag/Jahresmuseum, Murzzuschlag, Austria
Ecole Nationale des Beaux Arts de Bourges, Bourges, France
Galerie Johnen & Schottle, Cologne (with Elke Denda, Stefan Hablutzel and Daniel Oates)
1995 *Szenenwechsel V*, Museum für Moderne Kunst, Frankfurt/Main
Deutscher Pavillon, Venice Biennale (with Katharina Fritsch/Thomas Ruff)
Zwei und Zwanzig, Peter-Mertes-Stipendium 1985–1995, Bonner Kunstverein
Zimmerdenkmaler, Bochum
1996 The book is on the table, (with Tom Gidley, Siobhan Hapaska and Collier Schorr), Entwistle Gallery, London, England
Fondo, figura y lluvia, Galerie Antoni Estrany, Barcelona, Spain
Cabines de Bain, Piscine de La Motta, Fribourg, Switzerland
Elke Denda, Martin Honert, Zwei Editionen, Edition Opitz-Hoffmann, Bonn

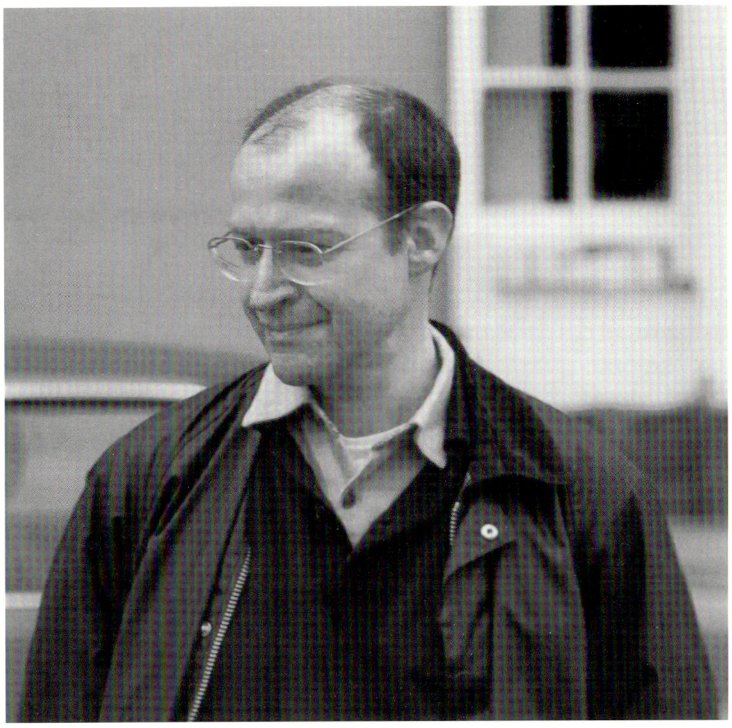

Private View. Contemporary British and German artists, The Bowes Museum, Barnard Castle, England
Views from Abroad – European Perspectives on American Art 2, Whitney Museum of American Art, New York, USA

THOMAS RUFF

1953 Born in Zell am Hannersbach, Schwarzwald
Studied at the Staatlichen Kunstakademie in Düsseldorf under Prof. Bernd Becher

Lives and works in Düsseldorf

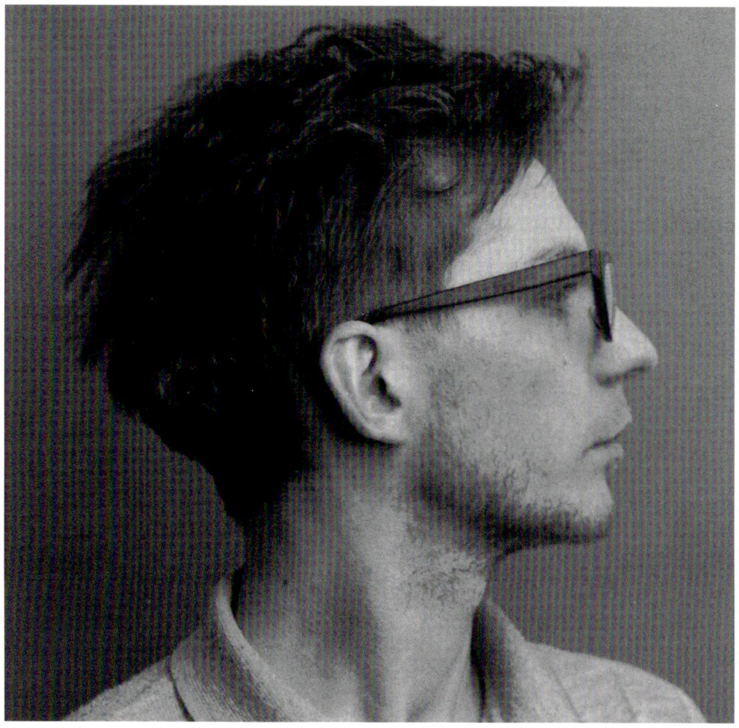

Solo Exhibitions

1981 Galerie Rudiger Schottle, Munich
1984 Galerie Rudiger Schottle, Munich
Galerie Konrad Fischer, Düsseldorf
1986 Galerie Philip Nelson, Lyon, France
1987 Galerie Johnen & Schottle, Cologne
Galerie Sonne, Berlin
Galerie Rudiger Schottle, Munich
Galerie Crousel-Robelin, Paris, France
1988 Museum Schloss Hardenberg, Velbert; Portikus, Frankfurt
Mai 36 Galerie, Luzern, Switzerland
Ydessa Hendeles Art Foundation, Toronto, Canada
1989 Galerie Bebert, Rotterdam, Netherlands
Cornerhouse, Manchester, England
Galerie Philip Nelson, Lyon, France
303 Gallery, New York, USA
XPO Galerie, Hamburg
Galerie Johnen & Schottle, Cologne
Fondation de Appel, Amsterdam, Netherlands
Galerie Rudiger Schottle, Munich
Galerie Pierre Huber, Genf, Switzerland
Portrats, Hauser, Sterne, Stedelijk Museum, Amsterdam, Netherlands
1990 *Portrats, Hauser, Sterne*, Centre National d'Art Contemporain – Le Magasin, Grenoble, France
Galerie Sonne, Berlin
Hauser, Mai 36 Galerie, Luzern, Switzerland
Stuart Regen Gallery, Los Angeles, USA
303 Gallery, New York
1991 Gallei Lia Rumma, Naples
Kunstverein Bonn
Galerie Rudiger Schottle, Munich
Galerie Johnen & Schottle, Cologne
1992 Galerie Rudiger Schottle, Munich
Kunstverein Braunschweig
Gallei Lia Rumma, Naples
Galerie Johnen & Schottle, Cologne
Kunstverein Bonn
Mai 36 Galerie, Luzern, Switzerland
1993 Galerie Johnen & Schottle, Cologne
Galerie Wilma Tolksdorf, Hamburg
DeWeer Art Gallery, Otegem
303 Gallery, New York
Mai 36 Galerie, Zürich
1994 303 Gallery, New York
Mai 36 Galerie, Zürich
Galerie Johnen & Schottle, Cologne
Galerie Rudiger Schottle, Munich
White Cube, London
1995 Galerie Wilma Tolksdorf, Hamburg
Galerie Johnen & Schottle, Cologne
Mai 36 Galerie, Zürich
Galerie Rudiger Schottle, Munich
1996 Fraenkel Gallery, San Francisco
303 Gallery, New York
Galerie Philip Nelson, Paris
Rooseum, Malmo

Selected Group Exhibitions

1988 *Aperto 88*, Venice Biennale
BiNationale, Kunstverein Düsseldorf, Museum of Fine Art, Boston
1989 Mit dem Fernrohr durch die Kunstgeschichte, Kunsthalle Basel
1991 metropolis, Martin-Gropius-Bau, Berlin
Architektur von Herzog & de Meuron, Venice Architectural Biennale
1992 Documenta 9, Kassel
1995 Szenenwechsel, Museum für Moderne Kunst, Frankfurt am Main

THOMAS SCHÜTTE

1954 Born in Oldenburg, West Germany
1973–81 Studied at Kunstakademie, Düsseldorf with Professor Fritz Schwegerand and Professor Gerhard Richter

Lives and works in Düsseldorf

Solo Exhibitions

1979	La Vitrine, Paris
	Galerie Arno Kohnen, Düsseldorf
1980	Galerie Rudiger Schottle, Munich
1981	Konrad Fischer, Düsseldorf
1982	Galerie Rudiger Schottle, Munich
1983	Konrad Fischer, Zürich
1984	Galerie Philip Nelson, Lyon
	Produzentengalerie, Hamburg
	Galerie Jean Bernier, Athens
	Galerie Jorg Johnen, Cologne
1985	Galerie Philip Nelson, Lyon
	Produzentengalerie, Hamburg
	Galerie Micheline Szwajcer, Antwerp
	Konrad Fischer, Düsseldorf
1986	Museum Haus Lange, Krefeld
	Galerie Rudiger Schottle, Munich
	Galerie Philip Nelson, Lyon
	Galerie Crousel-Hassenot, Paris
	Galerie Tucci Rosso, Turin
1987	Museum Overholland, Amsterdam
	Konrad Fischer, Düsseldorf
	Galerie Jean Berner, Athens
	Lichthof, Landesmuseum, Munster
	Galerie Micheline Szwajcer, Antwerp
1988	Galerie Philip Nelson, Lyon
	Staatliche Kunsthalle, Baden-Baden
	Galerie Christian Stein, Milan
	Galerie Tucci Rosso, Turin
1989	Marian Goodman Gallery, New York
	Musée de Clamecy, Clamecy
	Stichting de Appel, Amsterdam
	Portikus, Frankfurt am Main
	Galerie Pietro Sparta, Chagny
	Konrad Fischer, Düsseldorf
	Galerie Ute Parduhn, Düsseldorf
1990	Konrad Fischer, Düsseldorf
	Kunsthalle, Bern
	ARC/Musée d'Art Moderne de la Ville de Paris, Paris
	Stedelijk-van Abbemuseum, Eindhoven
	Marian Goodman Gallery, New York
	Galerie Rudiger Schottle, Munich
	Galerie Philip Nelson, Paris
	Galerie, Crousel BAMA, Paris
1991	Galerie Nelson, Lyon
	Kunstverein, Kassel
1992	Galerie Jean Bernier, Athens
	Konrad Fischer, Düsseldorf
	Antonio Tucci Rosso, Turin
	Galleria Frederica Inghilleri, Milan
	Raum fur Kunst, Hamburg

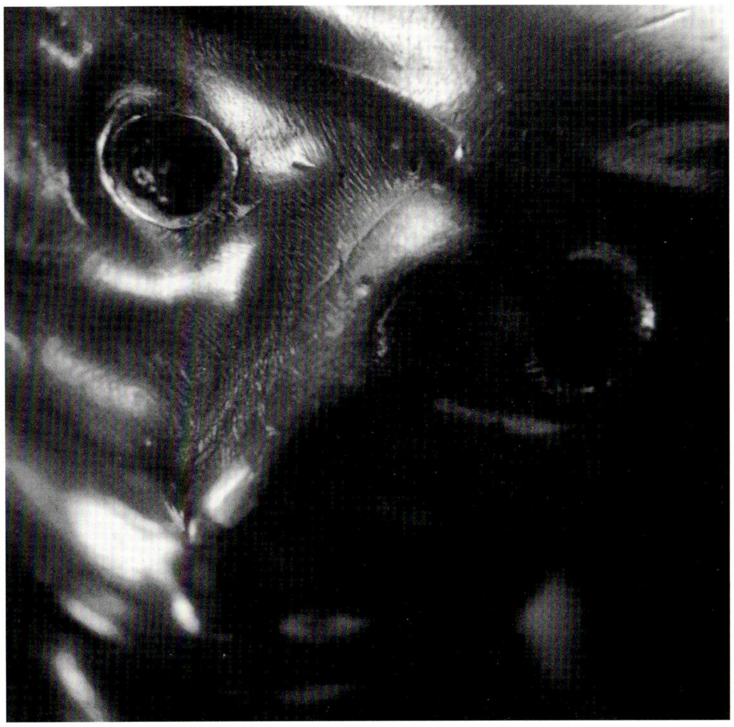

1993	Marian Goodman Gallery, New York
	Produzentengalerie, Hamburg
1994	Carre d'Art, Musée d'Art Contemporain, Nîmes
	Hamburger Kunsthalle, Hamburg
	Wurttembergischer Kunstverein, Stuttgart
	Galerie Philip Nelson, Paris
1995	Kunstraum Munchen e,V.
	Konrad Fischer, Düsseldorf
	Jean Bernier, Athens
	Centre Genovois de Gravure Contemporaine, Geneva
	Kunstverein, Munich
	Lisson Gallery, London
	Wako Works of Art, Tokyo
	St Annen Museum, Lubeck
	Galerie Tucci Rosso, Torre Pelice
1996	Marian Goodman Gallery, New York
	Leopold-Hoesch Museum, Duren
	Galerie Gebauer und Gunther, Berlin
	Kunstverein Wolfsburg
1997	Marian Goodman Gallery, New York

Selected Group Exhibitions

1991	*In anderen Raumen*, Museum Haus Lange und Haus Esters, Krefeld
	Inscapes, Stichting/Foundation De Appel, Amsterdam
1992	Documerita 9, Kassel
	Like Nothing Else in Tennessee, Serpentine Gallery, London
1993	*Briques*, Galerie Crousel-Robelin, Paris
1994	*Drawings*, Frith Street Gallery, London
1995	Le Nouveau Musée/Institut d'Art Contemporain, Villeurbanne
	Musée d'Art Contemporain, Bordeaux
	Museum Haus Lange, Krefeld, Germany
	Them and Us, Lisson Gallery, London

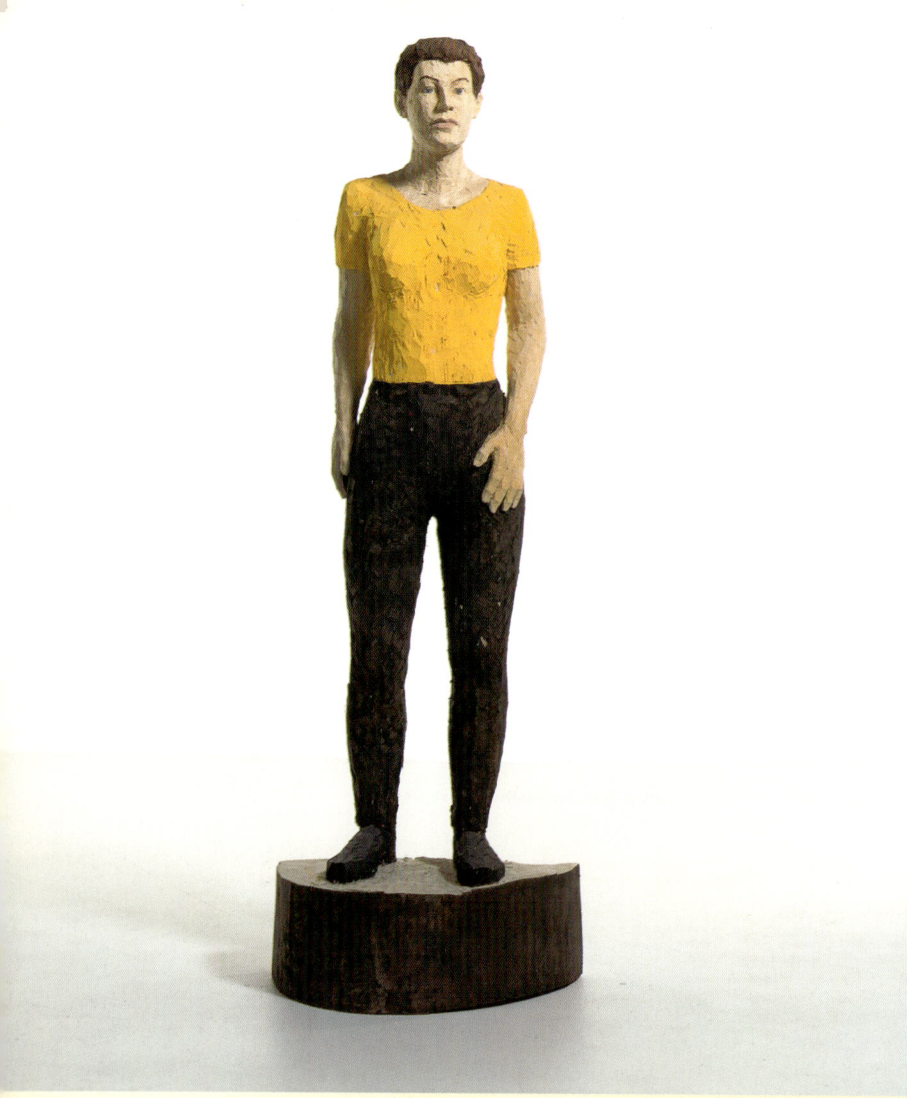
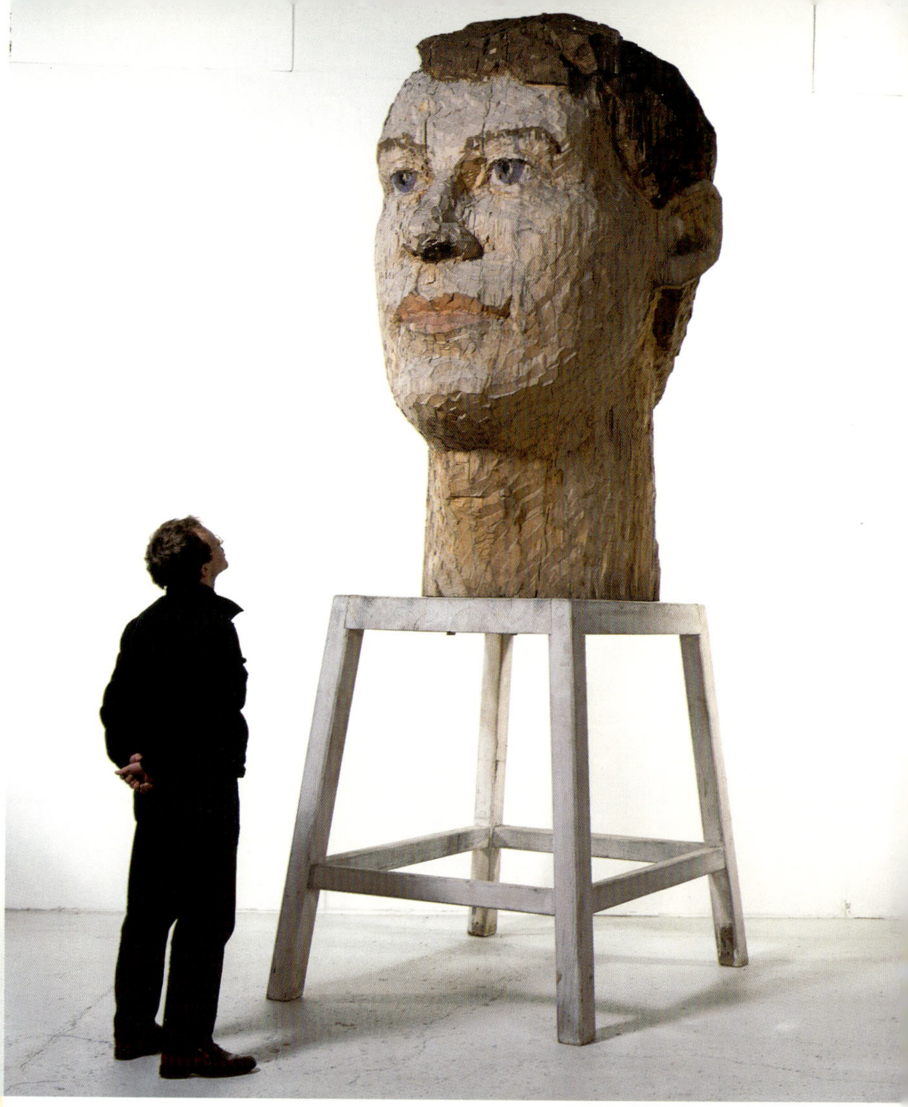
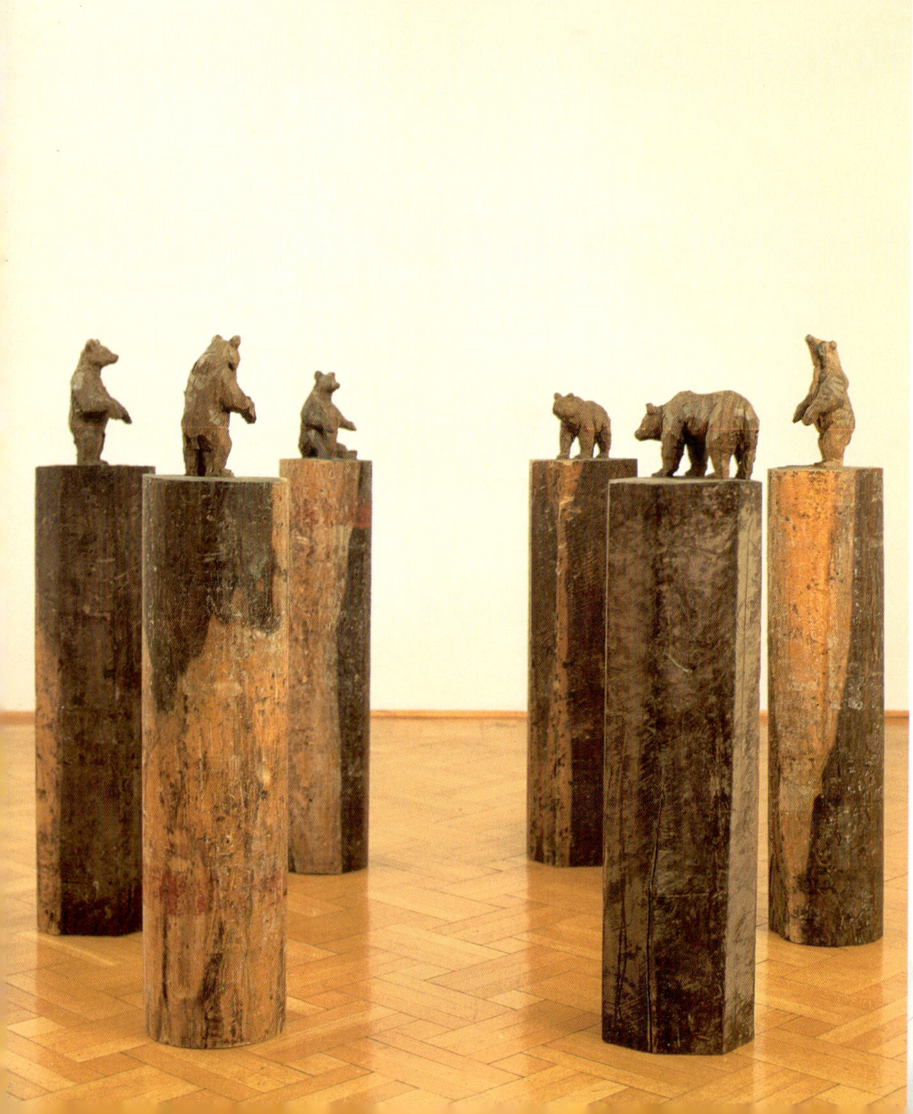
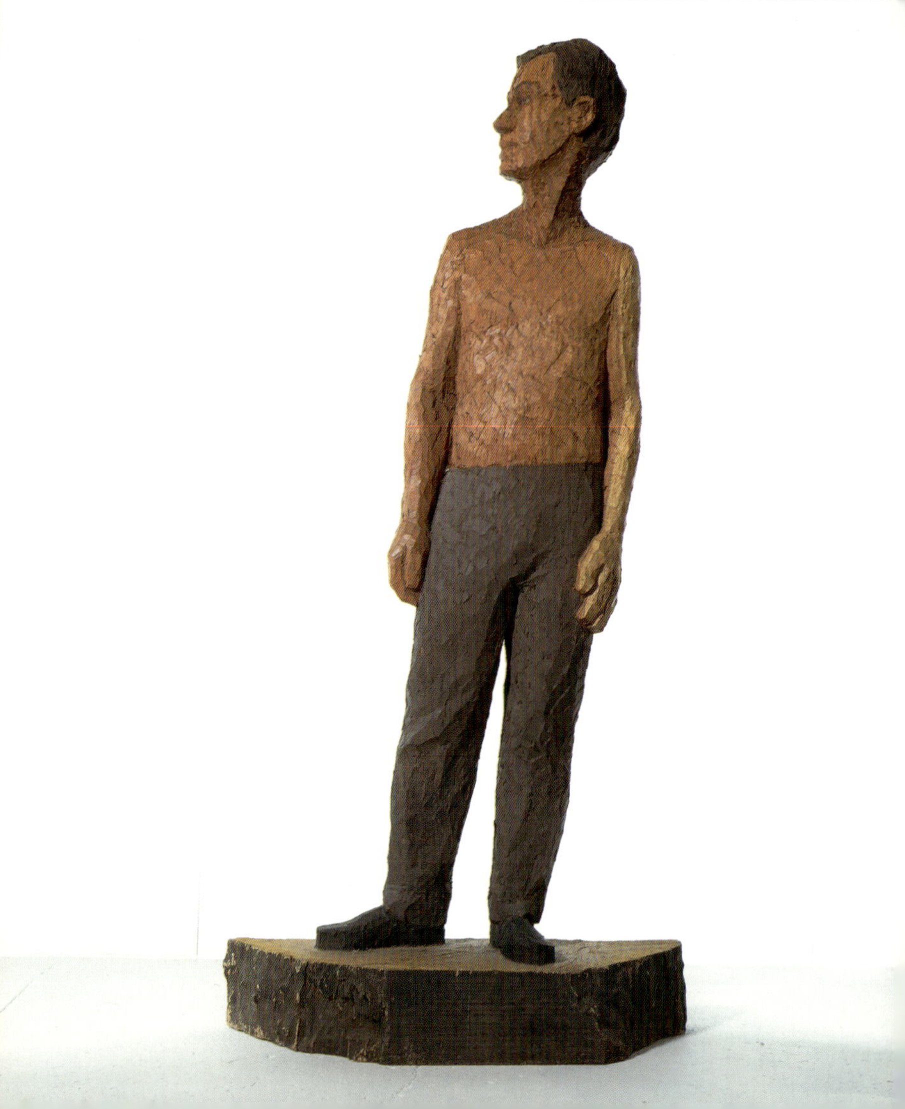

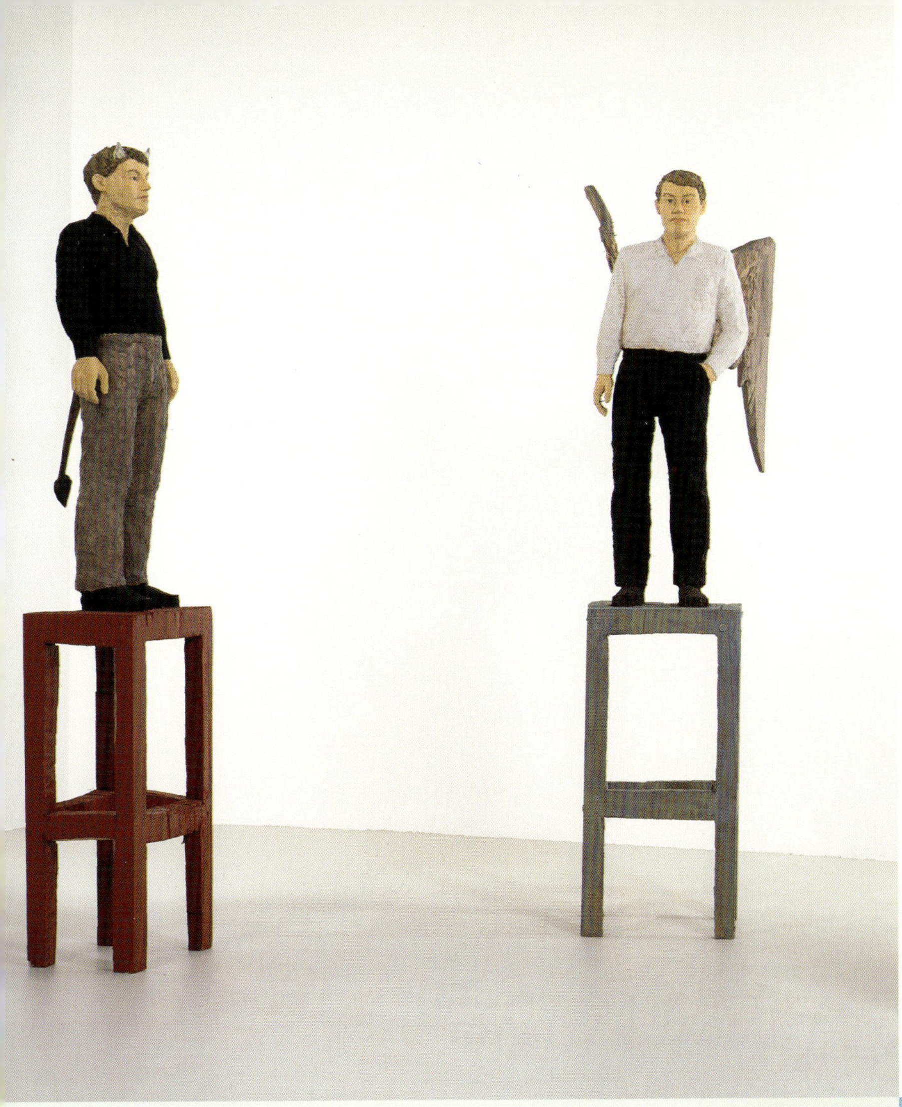

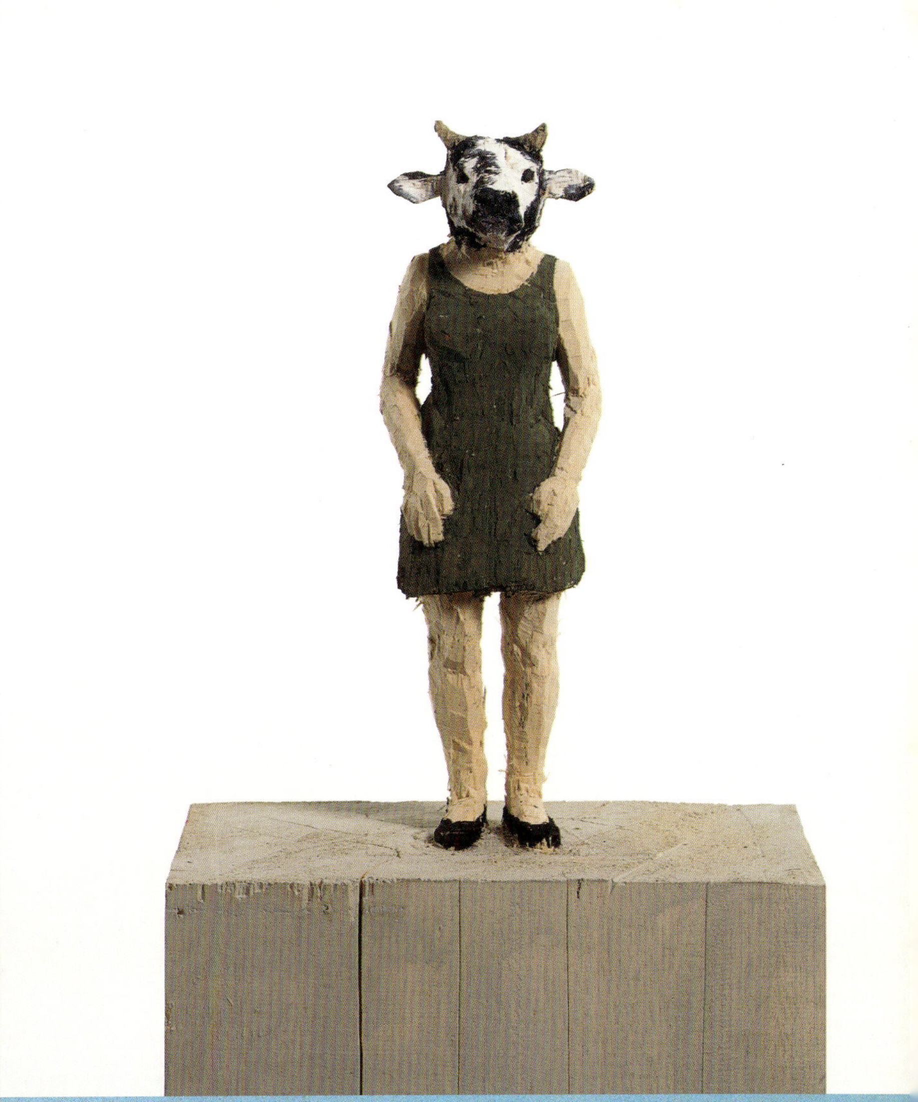

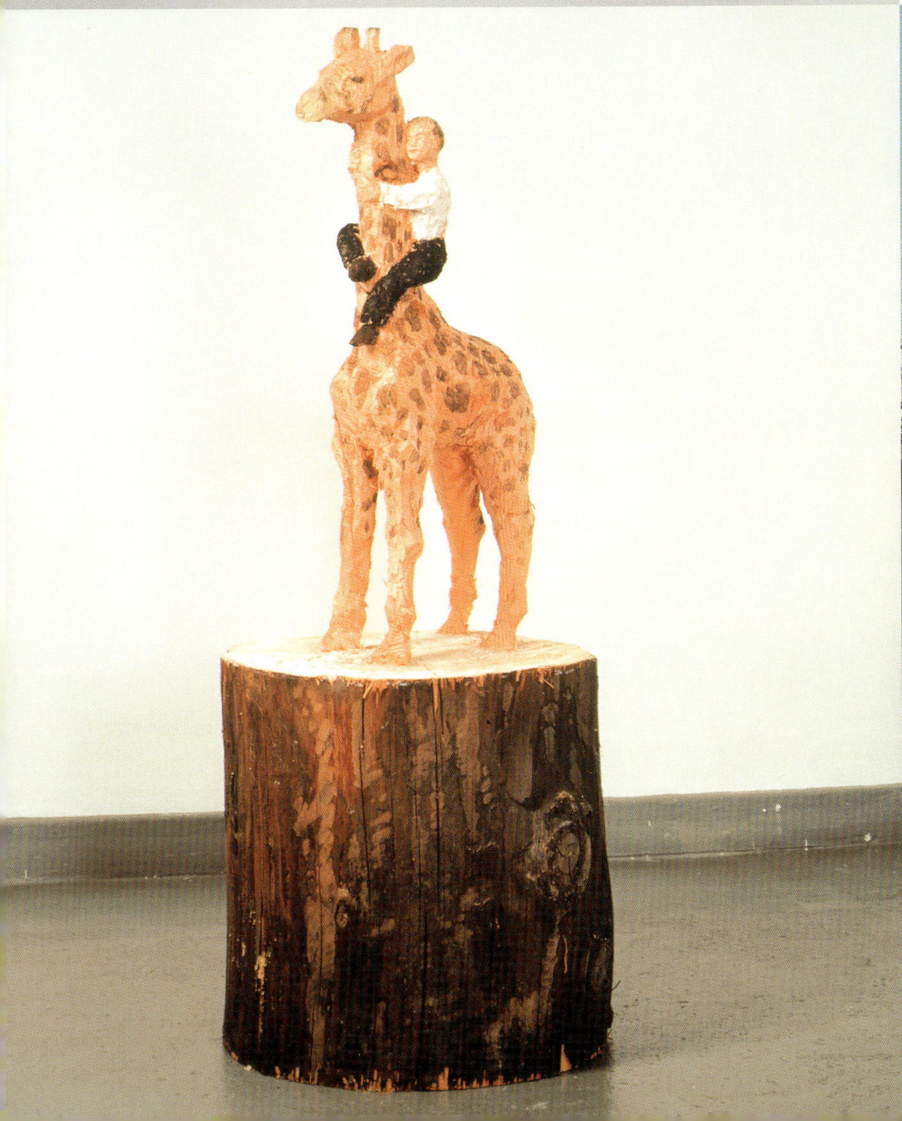

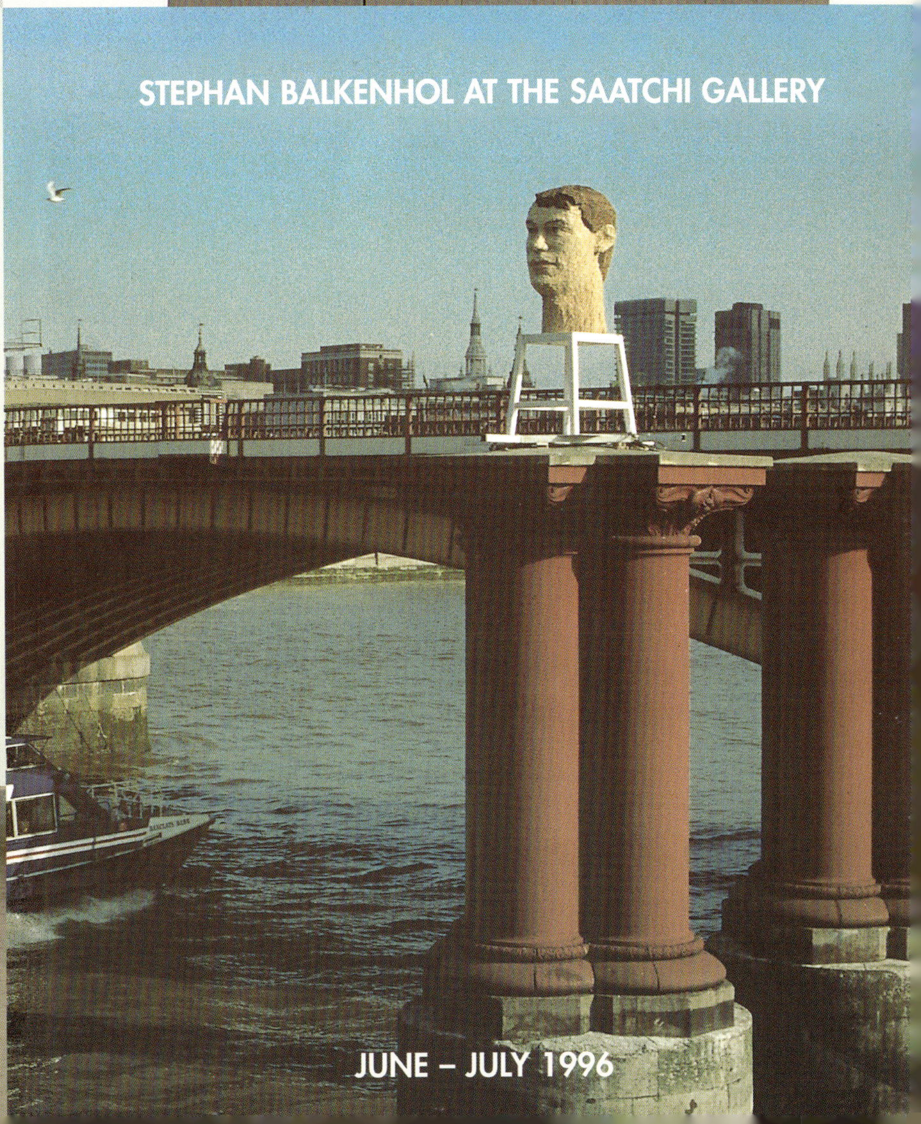
STEPHAN BALKENHOL AT THE SAATCHI GALLERY
JUNE – JULY 1996

Previous exhibitions at the Saatchi Gallery

March – October 1985	Donald Judd, Brice Marden, Cy Twombly, Andy Warhol
December 1985 – July 1986	Carl Andre, John Chamberlain, Dan Flavin, Sol LeWitt, Robert Ryman, Frank Stella
September 1986 – July 1987	Anselm Kiefer, Richard Serra
September 1987 – January 1988	New York Art Now (Part 1) Ashley Bickerton, Ross Bleckner, Robert Gober, Peter Halley, Jeff Koons,Tim Rollins & K.O.S., Haim Steinbach, Philip Taaffe, Meyer Vaisman
February – April 1988	New York Art Now (Part 2) Ashley Bickerton, Carroll Dunham, Robert Gober, Peter Halley, Ti-Shan Hsu, Jon Kessler, Jeff Koons, Allan McCollum, Peter Schuyff, Doug and Mike Starn
April – October 1988	Leon Golub, Philip Guston, Sigmar Polke, Joel Shapiro
November 1988 – April 1989	Jennifer Bartlett, Eric Fischl, Elizabeth Murray, Susan Rothenberg
April – October 1989	Robert Mangold, Bruce Nauman
November 1989 – February 1990	Leon Kossoff, Bill Woodrow
March – November 1990	Frank Auerbach, Lucian Freud, Richard Deacon
January – July 1991	Richard Artschwager, Cindy Sherman, Richard Wilson
September 1991 – February 1992	Mike Bidlo, Manuel Ocampo, Andres Serrano
March – October 1992	Young British Artists I John Greenwood, Damien Hirst, Alex Landrum, Langlands & Bell, Rachel Whiteread

October – December 1992	Out of Africa Contemporary African artists from the Pigozzi Collection
February – July 1993	Young British Artists II Rose Finn-Kelcey, Sarah Lucas, Marc Quinn, Mark Wallinger
September – December 1993	American Art in the 20th Century presented by The Royal Academy of Arts, London
February – July 1994	Young British Artists III Simon Callery, Simon English, Jenny Saville
September 1994	A Positive View 20th Century International Photography presented by Vogue
November 1994 – February 1995	Paula Rego, John Murphy, Avis Newman
April 1995 – June 1995	Young British Artists IV John Frankland, Marcus Harvey, Brad Lochore, Marcus Taylor, Gavin Turk
September – December 1995	Young British Artists V Glenn Brown, Keith Coventry, Hadrian Pigott, Kerry Stewart
January – May 1996	Young Americans Janine Antoni, Gregory Green, Jacqueline Humphries, Sean Landers, Charles Long, Tony Oursler, Richard Prince, Charles Ray, Kiki Smith
June – July 1996	Stephan Balkenhol
September – November 1996	Young British Artists VI Jordan Baseman, Daniel Coombs, Claude Heath, John Isaacs, Nina Saunders
January – March 1997	Fiona Rae and Gary Hume
April – July 1997	Duane Hanson

Acknowledgements

We gratefully acknowledge the kind assistance of the artists in putting together this catalogue.

We also wish to thank the following individuals and galleries:
Galerie Nelson, Johnen & Schöttle, Karsten Schubert, Mai 36 Galerie,
Marian Goodman Gallery, Monika Sprüth Galerie, 303 Gallery, Victoria Miro.

We extend sincere thanks to Greg Hilty who has written the essays.

We are also grateful to the following photographers for the use of photographic material:
Andreas Gursky, Thomas Powel, Friedrich Rosenstil, Thomas Ruff, Stephen White.

Designed and published in 1997 by
The Saatchi Gallery, 98a Boundary Road, London NW8 0RH.

Front cover detail of photograph of Thomas Schutte's *Grosser Geiste* 1996
courtesy of Thomas Powel.

Printed by The Pale Green Press Ltd.
Printed and bound in Great Britain.

ISBN 0 9527453 5 6